Praise for Voices Leading from the Ecotone

VOICES Leading from the Ecotone is a bold foray into the intersection of theory and practice within academia. Normore, Issa Lahera and Zoller challenge readers to explore the unbounded potential of "what if" as an embracing alternative to the stasis of "because." Anyone interested in being part of the future of education will find this a rich biome of ideas, irritations and illuminations.

~ *Timothy P. White, Chancellor, California State University, Long Beach CA*

Neither forest nor meadow, but tensions in the zone in between, are addressed by the authors examining hard-won growth from leadership energies in the highest- need schools in a large urban area. Normore, Issa Lahera, and Zoller brilliantly apply the concept of an ecotone to describe the experiences of leaders at all levels as they encounter and seek to improve the performance of teachers they work with. In each case, leaders unearth personal zones where they must overcome tensions in areas like their own values, beliefs, and leadership styles in order to successfully promote growth.

~ *Robert J. Garmston, Professor Emeritus, Education Leadership, California State University Sacramento*

Normore, Issa Lahera and Zoller have explored the crux of where real people, in real schools, solve real problems for the benefit of their school communities and the students they serve. In the purest expression of school leadership imaginable, these scholars attempt and succeed at revealing the thought processes that underlie genuine creative decision-making. This book is a must read for all concerned about our schools and those who lead them in their thoughts and actions on a daily basis.

~ *Professor Eric Nadelstern, Teachers College Columbia University, And former Deputy Chancellor of the NYC Public Schools*

Normore, Issa Lahera and Zoller use real stories from those who work the trenches to illustrate the Ecotone as a provocative and actionable pathway for taking the pain out of changing and mysticism out of change navigation. Reading this book has been eye opening and has energized me to act to in ways I never thought possible.

~ *Tarek B. Razik, Ed.D, Head of School, Jakarta Intercultural School Jakarta, Indonesia*

This timely book has struck at the heartland of educational leadership. Normore, Issa Lahera and Zoller have trusted the voices of those progressing school leadership every day to speak directly to readers. The narratives underscore the importance and ways of leading in pursuit of equity and social justice principles-often against the odds-to elevate students' life chances. Normore, Issa Lahera and Zoller bring applause to those who lead in schools for collective good with an exchange of ideas and strategies informed by sound practice, theory and research.

~ Pam Bishop, Ph.D, Associate Professor, Educational Leadership & Associate Dean, Graduate Programs, Western University, Ontario, Canada

The lively minds of these three authors have constructed, through the lens of the biological concept of ecotone, a thought provoking and behavior changing construct for school leadership.

~ Pete Pillsbury Sr., President, TargetSuccess, Inc.

Through the examination of practical experiences Normore, Issa Lahera and Zoller challenge us as educational leaders to step beyond what we know, and into the possibilities of what we can become.

~ Paul M. Marietti, Ed.D., Assistant Superintendent Pleasant Valley School District, Camarillo, CA

Drawing on real leaders' real stories of success and struggle, these authors weave a manuscript that will quickly become a must read for school leaders, especially those in challenging circumstances. It not only offers practical strategies and solutions for the multitude of challenges we face, it offers hope for a better future.

~Allan Walker, Chair Professor of International Educational Leadership, Education University of Hong Kong

In their book, *Voices Leading from the Ecotone*, Normore, Issa Lahera, and Zoller address an important problem of practice in the area of school leadership: how to tackle a series of real-world challenges by transforming what in some cases present as insurmountable obstacles into opportunities for personal and professional growth. This is quite an accomplishment, especially through the authors' use of narratives provided by actual educators. It is rare to find such a resource that effectively provides pragmatic ideas and functional tools that

are grounded in the lived experience of school leaders who, in many instances, work in the highest needs schools in the country. I highly recommend this book to current and aspiring leaders, including those who are committed to continuous improvement in their ability to navigate an increasingly complex educational landscape.
~ *Michael E. Spagna, Ph.D., Provost & Vice President for Academic Affairs, California State University, Dominguez Hills*

Normore, Issa Lahera and Zoller provide the reader up close and personal lens on the challenging work of leading educators who turn struggles into improved practices intended to address issues of social justice among disenfranchised students.
~*John Puglisi, Ph.D., Superintendent, Rio School District, Oxnard, CA*

One of the greatest challenges facing educators is the synthesis of new theories and their application in practice. In crafting Voices Leading from the Ecotone, Normore, Issa Lahera and Zoller blend the aspirational and practical in guiding readers through the complexities of change. Their respectful tone highlights the opportunities for personal growth that it can afford and reminds us that to create lasting change through initiatives that individuals truly invest in, they need to be supported and heard through the process. In a time of increased disruption, this book is a wonderful resource for leaders and for those mentoring the next generation of leaders.
~ *Brett Penny, Head of School, NIST International School, Wattana Bangkok, Thailand*

The printed press has enabled leadership scholars the ability to transform society while seeking consistency within normative organizational frameworks. Leadership in the digital age is truly complex. Normore, Lahera, and Zoller have brought together a collection of innovative writers who speak to the landscape of what can we know, will need to know, and how we lead in a way that may help temper the chaos we fear and cannot turn away from. Perhaps a common theme as within the an less predictable future leadership writers continue to prepare us.
~ *Kirk Anderson, Dean and Professor of Education, Memorial University, St. John's, Newfoundland, Canada*

VOICES

LEADING FROM THE ECOTONE

Anthony H. Normore

Antonia Issa Lahera

and

Kendall Zoller

Copyright © 2019 Word & Deed Publishing Incorporated

Voices Leading From The Ecotone

All rights reserved. Except as permitted under (U.S. Copyright Act of 1976), or (Canadian Copyright Act of 2012), no part of this publication may be reproduced, distributed, or transmitted in any form or by any means, or stored in a database or retrieval system, without prior written permission of the publisher.

Edited by Anthony H. Normore, Antonia Issa Lahera and Kendall Zoller
Copyediting: Ruth Bradley-St.-Cyr (Bradley-St.-Cyr & Associates, bradleystcyrassociates@gmail.com)
Book design by: bookdesign.ca

ISBN 978-0-9959782-6-3

Word & Deed Publishing Incorporated
434-2000 Appleby Line
Burlington, Ontario, Canada, L7L 7H7
(Toll Free) 1-866-601-1213
Visit our website at:
www.wordanddeedpublishing.com

Dedication and Acknowledgements

There are many unsung heroes joyously and tirelessly working in schools. It is to their positive spirits, resolve in the face of challenges, and everlasting quest for understanding that we dedicate this book. ISLI Fellows, you know this one is for you!

We wish to thank the diligent school leaders and teachers who shared their "aha" moments of innovative and creative leadership in support of effective teaching and learning. Our gratitude further extends to the US Department of Education, Office of Innovation and Improvement, for its support of the ISLI (Innovative School Leadership Initiative) Fellows program.

Contents

Praise for Voices Leading from the Ecotone i

Dedication and Acknowledgements. vii

Glossary of Acronyms xi

Foreword: Marty Linsky,
    Harvard University Kennedy School of Government xv

Preface 1

CHAPTER 1   **What is the Ecotone?** 5

CHAPTER 2   **Understanding the Hacking Framework** 17

CHAPTER 3   **Case Narratives** 23

    Case 3.1: Principal 26

    Case 3.2: Assistant Principal 31

    Case 3.3: Assistant Principal 34

    Case 3.4: Assistant Principal Secondary Counseling
        Services 38

    Case 3.5: Assistant Principal 41

    Case 3.6: Instructional Leadership Team. 45

    Case 3.7: Pupil Services and Attendance Counselor
        (PSA) 51

    Case 3.8: Assistant Principal 56

    Case 3.9: Assistant Principal 61

    Case 3.10: Chief Operating Officer. 64

    Case 3.11: Guidance Counselor. 68

    Case 3.12: Principal and ILT Team 70

    Case 3.13: Principal 74

    Case 3.14: Instructional Coach 78

    Case 3.15: Special Education Teacher 82

    Case 3.16: Assistant Principal 88

  Case 3.17: Assistant Principal 91
  Case 3.18: Executive Director/Chief Programs Officer . . .95
  Case 3.19: Instructional Coach 98
  Case 3.20: Teacher/Leadership/Math Chair 101
  Case 3.21: Principal 105
  Case 3.22: Principal 109
  Case 3.23: Principal 114
  Case 3.24: Principal 117
  Case 3.25: Resource Teacher/Instructional
        Leadership Team member 124
  Case 3.26: Science Instructional Lead 127
  Case #   132

CHAPTER 4 **Cases for Study** **133**

  Case 4.1: Assistant Principal 135
  Case 4.2: Assistant Principal 137
  Case 4.3: Assistant Principal 140
  Case 4.4: Counselor 145
  Case 4.5: Teacher and Instructional Coach 148
  Case 4.6: Principal 151
  Case 4.7: Teacher Resource Support Provider. 156
  Case 4.8: English Language Development Teacher . . . 159

References **165**

About the Editors. **169**

Glossary of Acronyms

ADA – Anti-Defamation League

AL – Adaptive Leadership

AP – Assistant Principal

ASCA - American School Counselors Association

BTSA – Beginning Teacher Support and Assessment

CAASPP – California Assessment of Student Performance and Progress

CASLA – Charter and Autonomous School Leadership Academy

CAST – Construction and Skilled Trades

CCSS – Common Core State Standards

CMO – Charter Management Organization

CST – California Standardized Testing

DACA – Deferred Action for Childhood Arrivals

DCFS – Department of Children and Family Services

DDI - Data-Driven Instruction

DOTS – District Office of Transition Services

EDI – Explicit Direct Instruction

ELA – English Language Arts

ELD- English Language Development

ELDT – English Language Development Test

ELL – English Language Learner

EO – Equal Opportunity

ESLO – Expected Student Learning Outcomes

EWA – Election to Work Agreement

GATE – Gifted and Talented Education

GEAR-UP - Gaining Early Awareness and Readiness for Undergraduate Programs

GPA – Grade Point Average

IDEA – Individuals with Disabilities Education Act

IDEIA – Individuals with Disabilities Education Improvement Act

IEP – Individual Education Plan

IFEF - Initially Fluent English Proficient

IL – Instructional Lead

ILT – Instructional Leadership Team

ISLI – Innovative School Leadership Institute

IT – Informational Technology

LRE – Least Restrictive Environment

LTEL - Long Term English Learner

MSA - Male Success Alliance

NGSS - Next generation Science Standards

PBIS – Positive Behavioral Interventions and Supports

PD – Professional Development

PLC – Professional Learning Community

PSA – Pupil Services and Attendance

PSC – Public School Choice

PUC - Partnership to Uplift Communities

RFEP - Reclassified Fluent English Proficient

RP – Restorative Practices

RST/RSP – Resource Specialist Teacher/Program

RTI – Response to Intervention
SBA - Standards-Based Grading or School-Based Assessment
SBAC – Smarter Balanced Assessment Consortium
SCC – School-Coordinating Council
SDC – Special Day Class
SDP – School Development Plan
SLP – School Leadership Program
SPED – Special Education
SSPT - Student Success and Progress Team
SSR - Sustained Silent Reading
SST – Student Support Team
STEM – Science, Technology, Engineering and Math
TDQ – Text Dependent Question
TPS – Temporary Protected Status
TSP – Targeted Student population
UHS – Urban High School
WASC – Western Association of Schools and Colleges
YPI - Youth Policy Institute

Foreword

Leave it to Antonia Issa Lahera, Kendall Zoller, and Anthony Normore to redefine the word "hacking" from a pejorative meaning to a noble one. If anyone could pull that off, they can. What they have done with this book is to hack the world of leadership development successfully, in a roughly parallel fashion to what they are hoping their readers will do in the worlds they inhabit.

For these three, the terrain they occupy is the area of overlap between the world of leadership theory and the world of practice. They have created their own ecotone, with a foot in each camp. Hacking leadership in the ecotone flows out of their professional consulting and training work, primarily with principals and senior administrators at some of the nation's most troubled public schools. It flows out of their own passion and commitment to those educators and the children they serve. Most importantly, their work — and this book — comes from their observation and frustration that the current leadership literature, theories, and tools are not adequate for those admirable men and women seeking to inform and reform distressed public schools in disadvantaged communities, some of the most intractable, entrenched systems in existence.

Toni, Kendall, and Tony are well positioned to be disrupters. They have operated on the fringes of academia and the world of practice without being owned by either. They are therefore free to look at the multiple streams of university-based leadership theory and take one idea from column A, one from column B, and so on, without being slaves to the arcane rules and practices of academic publishing, promotion, and tenure. Similarly, they are not school principals immersed in specific environments. They are free to theorize about what mixture of ideas from the leadership corpus might actually be stirred together to create a stew that will be greater than the sum of its ingredients. This freedom provides a way of thinking and operating that has the promise (or at least the potential) of arming the many dedicated, overworked, underpaid educators with better resources for leading transformation.

They have drawn from literally every respected leadership theory they could get their hands on. They have also taken guidance from such works as *Design Thinking* and *Immunity to Change*, which are not strictly in the leadership development field but provide helpful insights. And they have artfully integrated Kendall's groundbreaking earlier work on communicative intelligence (CI), making it a cornerstone of a broader, overarching approach. They will undoubtedly get pushback from narrow, defensive academics protecting their turf and from exhausted, discouraged educators claiming the authors do not understand what they are up against. This will be a good indicator of a successful hack.

Whether hacking leadership in the ecotone will become the new standard of leadership development or education reform will not be clear until some courageous principals and school administrations try out these strategies. For now, all we know is that the authors have broken ground and given people committed to deep change a new way of approaching their complex challenges.

If you are one of those people, read this book. Run hacking leadership experiments. And let Kendall, Toni, and Tony know how it goes.

They have hacked the system. You can, too.

As a willing and enthusiastic hackee, I am glad they did.

—*Marty Linsky, New York, July 10, 2018*

Marty Linsky is a professor at the Harvard University Kennedy School of Government and a co-founder, with Ronald A. Heifetz, of Cambridge Leadership Associates. He has published extensively on leadership, management, politics, and education.

Preface

Standing at the edge of the forest, you look across the meadow. Or, standing at the edge of the meadow you look into the forest. Sometimes the boundary between the forest and meadow is succinct and well defined. At other times, the forest seems to infiltrate the meadow and the meadow seems to infiltrate the forest. This area of infiltration is an *ecotone*.

The ecotone is a place of tension where survival is tested in unique ways. The adaptations that plants and animals have in the forest may not be useful in the ecotone. The same is true for the plants and animals of the meadow as they venture into the ecotone. The ecotone is not forest; it is not meadow; it is a place with greater diversity than either one. In terms of school leadership, the ecotone is where we seek necessary and essential adaptation.

Where you are now, both professionally and organizationally, is not a place where leadership is necessary. You are already *there*. Nor do we see leadership as necessary for where you want to be, as it is not yet real. Leadership, the act of leading, is needed to traverse the place between where you are and where you want to be. That place is an ecotone.

To lead into and through the ecotone means embracing uncertainty. It means giving up what you once believed to be essential and embracing what you thought expendable. It means shifting your mental perspectives to embrace turbulence and unpredictability. White water rafting, for example, is not about the calm waters; it is about roiling waters, unpredictability, challenge, and endurance. We choose to white water raft. Let's choose to traverse the ecotone with the anticipation of pleasure, challenge, and success. Let's rely on courage, humility, resilience, and cooperation. Leading alone is delusional. Leading with intention through the ecotone to a desired state — a state of many possibilities — is the seed for creativity and innovation.

Creativity and innovation are mobilized by disruptions to the system, to our habits, to our current ways of thinking. The emerging innovations are then used for "hacking" the system. Hacking is the implementation of small perturbations created in the ecotone to initiate and implement change in the system. When we take others on a journey into and through an ecotone, they may experience what they have never experienced before. They adapt in ways they once thought impossible. To adapt is to be creative and innovative.

We wrote this book for readers who care deeply about school leadership, appreciate its strengths and imperfections, and are committed to making it better. If you are comfortable with the status quo and aspire to no more than a job, or if you believe that nothing short of a revolution can save an industry in jeopardy, this is not your book. If you strive to be a leader with impact and become a significant force for good, we hope you find in these pages a readable, intellectually provocative, pragmatic approach to your work and its possibilities. The contributing authors do some of the most important work in the world today. They are hardworking, highly motivated, and deeply committed to improving teaching, learning, and leading for healthy and vibrant school communities where all involved in the learning process can flourish.

School leadership is a highly social endeavor. The collaboration and partnerships needed to get things done foster a sense of community, connection, and shared purpose. There is deep excitement and satisfaction in seeing tangible, measureable outcomes from one's efforts. But along with its benefits, school leadership brings challenges and even heartaches, particularly in an era of political controversy, public doubt, technological change, demographic shift, mission drift, and financial crisis. School leadership is demanding work that tests the mind, soul, and stamina of all who attempt it. We know because we have done it, and we have worked with many others over the years to help them learn to do it better. We have studied the factors that make the work so difficult, written about them, and benefitted from the research of colleagues in the field.

Schools constitute a special type of organization; its complex mission, dynamics, personnel structures, and values require a distinct set of understandings and skills to lead and manage them well. This book aims to provide ideas, tools, and encouragement to help readers make better sense of their work and their learning institutions, feel more confident, and become more adaptive, skilled, and versatile in handling the vicissitudes of daily school life.

Our approach builds from multiple sources. The narratives included in this book are primarily practical in nature and drawn from school leaders at the highest needs schools in a large urban school district in the southwestern United States. Every day they grapple with social justice and equity: poverty, gangs, violence, racial tension, disability, and LGBTQ issues. Each narrative highlights a leader's struggles, challenges, and the "a-ha" moments that help the school move forward.

Our collective K–16 experience as educators of teaching and leading are informed by serving as teacher, instructional coach, vice principal, principal, and district office leader. We have studied, lived, and worked in private and urban public institutions in the United States, Canada, and elsewhere in the world where demographic diversity flourishes. We have held positions in higher education as tenured professor, program coordinator, department chair, federal grants director, program director, and as regional, national, and international consultants. Many of these roles reflect our experience in teaching leadership training, development, and preparation to aspiring professionals in graduate courses and to experienced administrators in executive programs and summer institutes.

We hope the narratives in this book reflect all that we have observed and learned from our colleagues, our students, their school communities, and their experiences as we continue to navigate that area of infiltration, creativity, and innovation known as the ecotone.

Anthony H. Normore
Antonia Issa Lahera
Kendall Zoller

Chapter 1

What is the Ecotone?

The ecotone is a place rich in diversity between two or more communities of people, ideas, values, and beliefs. Here, relationships and creativity thrive to design innovations and address enduring challenges. In order for leaders to lead effectively from the ecotone, they need specific skills that help them to innovate and create. They need a space and a place to help figure things out. From related research, it is clear that leaders must be astute in creating relationships, must connect to emotional intelligence and self-awareness, must use communicative intelligence, must know themselves, their values, their biases, and their triggers, must know those who surround them, and must be able to identify and diagnose individual, collaborative, and adaptive challenges. To this end, the narratives in this book provide leadership experiences shared by those who understand the critical components for effectiveness in both discourse and practice. Their individual experiences are drawn from one of three types of ecotones: 1) *thrust into something new*, 2) *been here before*, and 3) *create your own*.

Drawing from biology, an ecotone is the transition area between two biomes. This transition area gives rise to a new community. Organisms move back and forth from one ecosystem to the other. The ecotone between ecosystems has greater biodiversity, competition, and tension than the surrounding ecosystems. The more diversity and the greater number of components, the more energy in the system. In the ecotones of nature, diversity is heightened since species from both neighboring communities may live in this in-between space along with unique species that do not exist in the neighboring ecosystems.

In human terms, we have borrowed the concept of "ecotone" to denote a space where we can grapple with challenges and devise potential solutions. New perspectives that do not exist in the neighboring ecosystems exist in the ecotone, thus providing an important reason to do work there. Since we exist in multiple communities and ecotones, we can go wittingly or unwittingly to them as challenges emerge. Another way to describe this would be cross-pollination.

Types of Ecotones

We propose three types of leadership ecotones. There may be more; however, for our purposes, for the sake of simplicity and adaptive agility, three seem to work out well. The first is the ecotone you are *thrust into* because of an immediate circumstance. It might be while sitting in a meeting and realizing that chaos is bubbling up and forcing instability. These can be accusations of project ineptitude, emerging time limitations, internal conflict produced by the dynamics of those on the team. In any case, you are there, and you are *thrust into* action.

The second type of ecotone includes the places you have *been before*. These may be places you enjoy going to because they worked in the past. They are the places where past challenges were successfully navigated. Or they can be familiar places of chaos that you have been to before that did not work. They simply are not new. This is the ecotone where challenges keep showing up as they have before.

A third ecotone is one of your own choosing or creating. It is the ecotone *you create* because you see an opportunity to move towards your destination. Leading from this ecotone is satisfying because when you choose to create it and enter into it, you often get to choose who comes with you, what to bring, and how to navigate it. This ecotone is akin to those times when you choose to go white water rafting. You may be uncertain about what the ride will be like, but you are prepared physically and mentally.

All three ecotones have much in common. There is chaos, unpredictability, instability, often moving targets, and you know many people will experience discomfort, uneasiness, and trepidation. Courage, resiliency, humility, and strength of relationships are required in all three ecotones. How people interact and develop their new relationships contributes significantly to their success in navigating the ecotone. These new associations and the emerging innovations are then used for "hacking" the system. In this case, "hacking" means the testing of innovations as small perturbations by those in the ecotone in order to create and implement change. People working together make the difference. What we know, what we can do, and how we feel are the choices we make in the ecotones.

Social Justice Leadership Orientation

Concept labels such as moral, servant, social justice, value-added, ethical, equity, diversity, and cultural leadership attempt to provide a roadmap to wise, ethical, social justice oriented decision-making in a complex, ever-changing world. This process is different from empirical research. Instead, scholars have chosen specific words and phrases to support newer ideas, developing names for leadership styles that mirror current cultures, and at the same time connect with social science research. This connection links leadership theory and social science research, ultimately addressing demands for social justice in the more permanent structures of society such as governments and schools (Beyer, 2012, p. 2).

The most recent theoretical concepts found in educational and organizational leadership literature point to the need to more clearly define the connections between educational leadership and social justice in our educational systems (Beyer, 2012, p. 7). Consequently, principals can fail to identify the best possible decision because 1) they lack the cognitive capacity to consider all possible alternatives, 2) they are subjected to influences and pressures, and 3) they struggle with organizational uncertainty and legitimacy. Thus, a principal's social justice orientation or worldview is necessary and important to the creation of more socially just schools, but not sufficient given the complexity of schools and the decisions that must be made (DeMatthews, Mungal, & Carrola, 2015, p. 18). When principals are forced to make choices about school staffing, curricula, program development, and budgeting, contend DeMatthews and colleagues (2015), significant tensions can arise. These choices may be forced by timelines and policy mandates, with significant implications for particular groups of students, cutting through the intersectionality of marginalized groups, and potentially providing equity to some but not all (DeMatthews et al., 2015, p. 21).

Key themes surface from the literature upon which social justice school leaders must focus. First, the idea of a desirable or undesirable choice must be driven by values aligned with the beliefs of the principal and the community. Second, ethical principles must direct decision-making processes by reframing problems and establishing new possibilities. Third, social justice-oriented principals need soft skills (communicative intelligence) to conduct decision analysis processes. Fourth, principals must critically reflect on power, privilege, and inequities in society if they wish to lead for social justice. This includes looking inwards at themselves, their leadership practices, their decisions, and their actions. Finally, rational models of decision-making place a high degree of control with the decision maker, as if that person can control the decision-making situation and context. Many principals do not have the time, resources, or capacity to obtain all the information needed to make a rational choice. The competing social objectives of different stakeholders across different social justice issues also limit the potential alternatives (see DeMatthews et al., 2015, p. 28).

The ecotone you choose to create can be the breeding ground for innovations that can be tested and refined to address the challenges of social justice. It is necessary to enter the ecotone in order to access this creative space; if you remain in the existing system, too many factors inhibit innovation since the system is designed *not* to change. Entering the ecotone space allows for initial disruptions and creativity to emerge without being inhibited by the implacable force of inertia in the larger system. The ecotone, therefore, is the creative laboratory for innovation.

Emotional Intelligence (EI)

Emotional intelligence is important. Individuals with high EI characteristics generally have better health and wellbeing; they are also are more effective leaders. There are a number of constructs and definitions of what EI is exactly and how it should be measured or viewed. Examining specific components of EI — such as self-regulation, self-awareness, awareness of others' emotions, and regulation of others' emotions — may be more useful than muddy constructs. EI is "trainable" and can be improved. The body of literature on the relationship between EI and leadership styles shows that transformational leaders tend to have higher EI than transactional leaders.

Though initially EI was a controversial concept, over the last 25 years it appears to have be more accepted and associated with effective leadership (Boyatzis & Saatcioglu, 2008). Multiple longitudinal studies of MBA students who complete a program designed to improve their EI were examined by Boyatzis and Saatcioglu (2008). They concluded that although EI can be improved, different approaches to developing EI may have differential effects. They argued that a holistic approach to developing EI was more effective than a narrow approach, specifically contrasting development across knowledge, competencies, and values versus simply across knowledge.

Although EI is strongly associated with effective leadership, exactly how EI is defined and how it connects with leadership is poorly defined. Researchers have argued that "emotional intelligence, especially the abilities to perceive emotions accurately, understand the causes of emotions, use emotions to facilitate thinking and decision making, and regulating emotions" are particularly important for effective leaders (Caruso, Fleming, & Spector, 2014, pp. 97–98). Grobler, Moloi, and Thakhordas (2016) examined how different EI leadership styles affected teachers' perspectives of the implementation of newly mandated curriculum. The study found that teachers were more likely to implement the curriculum when their school leader exhibited EI traits such as building culture around the deployment of the curriculum rather than saying that the curriculum was mandated by the state. The authors suggest that school leaders receive training and development in EI to facilitate changes in schools. Moore (2009) makes the case for a link between successful student outcomes and school leadership. Further, characteristics of high EI are linked to high performing principals, suggesting that principals would benefit from coaching or development of IE as a productive way to improve school outcomes. Nelis, Quoidbach, Mikolajczak, and Hansenne (2009) conducted a small study where half the participants received EI training and the other half did not. Those who received training improved their EI, versus those who did not, and their improved EI persisted for at least six months after the completion of the training.

Patti, Holzer, Brackett, and Stern (2015) examined the development and implementation of a coaching program designed to prepare instructional coaches to conduct professional development to improve EI. Twelve coaches were followed for two years. Overall findings suggest that both the coaches and the participants improved their EI as a result of the professional development. The study, however, cites lack of support from school leadership as a factor undermining the development of the program. Another study focused on Intelligence Quotient (IQ) and Emotional Quotient (EQ) on cross-border leadership and its level of effectiveness globally. Rockstuhl, Seiler, Ang, Van Dyne, and Hubert (2011) looked at the EI of Swiss military officers as a proxy for cultural intelligence, which the authors argue is an important dimension for those doing cross-border work. This idea led us to wonder about how more multicultural leadership in US schools and businesses would also transform them. Such questions were also taken up by Schutte, Malouff, Thorsteinsson, Bhullar, and Rooke (2013), who explored interventions to increasing EI across a number of realms, from schools to large organizations. They suggest that EI can be improved through training and that the training itself can have a positive effect on participants, specifically that participants may be more persistent in completing school, or that EI can improve morale in work environments.

Finally, researchers argue that although there are multiple constructs of EI, it should be integrated into leadership programs to improve the EI of leaders (Sadri, 2012). A number of curricular programs for students have been created in schools around the idea of EI, but they are generally very broad in their approach and definition of EI. These programs include self-awareness curriculum, communicative abilities, and a broad "character development" curriculum (Bar-On, 2010). The communicative abilities of EI include the following: 1) establishing and maintaining credibility; 2) establishing rapport (easy to do with those who think like you, more challenging otherwise); 3) how to listen, acknowledge, and respond; and 4) how to recover with grace when the intended message is not aligned with the perceived message. The skills for these abilities are found in Communicative Intelligence (CI; Zoller, 2015).

Cultural Competency, Communication, and Commitment

Other research have focused on content knowledge and the need for school leaders to pursue candidates who reflect such qualities as the following, known as the 3 C's: 1) cultural competency, including cultural awareness, experience, and understanding; 2) communication skills bridging urban teaching and learning; and 3) commitment to serve the students and the community (Khalil & Brown, 2015, p. 80). While cultural awareness and communication both involve knowledge and skills, commitment is a disposition, which may be challenging to develop, because it is essentially a component of a teacher's personality (Khalil & Brown, 2015, p. 86). To provide equitable teaching and learning opportunities, school leaders must apply these 3 C's to lead for social justice (Khalil & Brown, 2015, p. 87).

As public school students become increasingly more diverse and poorer, the 21st century reality of changing public school demographics in the US will demand school leaders who embrace and uphold the tenets of school leadership for social justice to ensure that all students have equal access to high-quality education. More likely than not, a large percentage of principals today have very little connection to the histories and cultures of the students with whom they interact. This paradox of cultural incongruence, many researchers would argue, has resulted in a disconnect that exacerbates the achievement gaps, disproportionate student discipline, and high school dropout rates in the US (Kemp-Graham, 2015, p. 100). School leadership is complex; quite often school leaders must negotiate numerous sociopolitical and sociocultural issues that they have not been trained to handle (Kemp-Graham, 2015, p. 101).

School leaders have yet to realize that to make systemic change for marginalized students, they must first understand their own biases, acknowledge their own deficit thinking, and engage in ongoing critical reflection on their own beliefs of oppression and social justice. This process of becoming aware of the cultural influences in school settings and of our own biases that perpetuate inequitable practices within schools is essential in order to transform them (Kemp-Graham, 2015, p. 102). In order to prepare aspiring leaders to be school-ready principals leading 21st century schools that advocate for the success of all students, principal preparation programs will need to overhaul the current curriculum. The revised curriculum ought to focus on building understanding of and achieving mastery of critical theories related to culture, disability, ethnicity, gender, and language as well as understanding patterns of discrimination, inequity, injustice, and the benefits and liabilities associated with individual groups (Kemp-Graham, 2015, p. 125).

Professional Preparation

Given the differences in professional preparation for school counselors and principals, as well as the lack of emphasis in their training on working collaboratively, other research examined the different perceptions of school counselors and principals regarding their relationship, leadership, and professional preparation (Armstrong, MacDonald, & Stillo, 2010, p. 5). Among the key findings was this: if a secondary school counselor who is not satisfied with the status quo initiates a conversation with a principal who is satisfied with the status quo, the counselor faces a more difficult challenge than one whose perceptions more closely match her principal's (Armstrong et al., 2010, p. 14). Moreover, one of the challenges that many school counselors experience involves initiating conversations with principals that may include elements of conflict. Thus, being assertive may be more challenging for female school counselors who have a strong dislike for conflict. Based on the findings of this study, the need to be assertive with principals is even more critical in secondary schools because the perception gap between counselors and principals is much more pronounced (Armstrong et al., 2010, p. 17).

The argument being advanced here is that an ideal future state can be envisioned and acted upon. Through educational leadership, social influence can be used to shape school cultures and practices, which in turn support greater equity in learner outcomes and future decisions (Forde & Torrance, 2017, p. 3). Experiential learning processes — particularly coaching, mentoring, and collaborative learning — help strengthen personal qualities to enable leaders to seek and commit to change. Other skillsets also need to be developed — ones that acknowledge and prepare school leaders for the political processes they will have to navigate to bring about change. There is a fine line between being political and simple expediency, so there is a further dimension to consider (Forde & Torrance, 2017, p. 17).

Balancing Hope and Resistance

The ideal of social justice for all learners is a weighty one. School leaders must balance the hope inscribed in a vision of inclusion and equality with a resilience to tackle barriers and resistance. From this discussion, a number of aspects have emerged as significant in social justice leadership regarding leaders' knowledge and understanding of issues related to equality and social justice, their own position and sense of purpose, and the skillset needed to work for social justice across the school community (Forde & Torrance, 2017, p. 18). Much rests on school leadership to foster the conditions for effective learning for the diverse group of learners in the school. Leadership development has a vital role to play in developing the required understandings, skills, and stance for social justice leadership. To enable school leaders to generate longer term strategies, leadership development must be seen as a transformational experience that fosters leadership dispositions geared to social justice (Forde & Torrance, 2017, p. 21).

One example comes from a study that focused on the relationship between a social justice curriculum and the dispositions of graduate students enrolled in an online pre-service school principal preparation program (Allen, Harper, & Koschoreck, 2017, p. 1). The researchers found that there was indeed a positive shift in the development of their students' dispositions in the following five areas: 1) promoting the common good over personal interests, 2) seeing diversity as an asset, 3) providing a safe and supportive learning environment, 4) ensuring learning for every student, and 5) building on diverse social and cultural assets (Allen et al., 2017, pp. 7–8).

Adaptive Leadership

One emergent leadership model, adaptive leadership, sees multiple leaders (i.e., teachers, school administrators) sharing responsibility for accomplishing tasks (Squires, 2015, p. 15). The complex challenges facing education require solutions generated by multiple stakeholders through collaborative processes. Such collaborative cultures and collective efficacy in developing solutions, in turn, require adaptive leadership. Through intentional development of strong collaborative structures and processes, adaptive leaders move beyond distributive leadership toward a more efficacious leadership style needed to tackle the increasingly complex, adaptive problems in education (Heifetz & Linsky, 2009; Squires, 2015). Key understandings and valued tenets of open collaboration include the following:

- **Relationship capital**: the quality of interpersonal connections and relationships is integral to the collaboration
- **Reciprocal/co-planned**: all participants create the goals and content of sessions

- **Constructed/organic**: authentic meaning making occurs when participants create appropriate lessons, sessions, and units for the situation
- **Job-embedded/sustained**: on-the-job learning opportunities are contextualized and applied throughout the school day (Kang, 2016, p. 50)

Teachers do not simply want resources given to them. They often seek out relationships from more knowledgeable or experienced colleagues to ask advice, model lessons, or start an inquiry group. Establishing relationships within collaboration is essential for learning and knowledge development (Kang, 2016, p. 51). The data revealed that it takes time and effort to build rapport and trust in adaptive and collaborative relationships. Additionally, although collaboration and adaptive challenges involved a lot of work from both parties, in the end it was well worth it (Kang, 2016, p. 52).

A Brief Example of a *VOICE Leading from the Ecotone*

At a small pilot high school in one of the poorest, most marginalized communities in South Los Angeles, an instructional coach identified the adaptive challenge as a failure to complete assignments, and failure in classes. The coach's mantra for leading is *students first, content second*. The coach states, "I believe it is important to see my students for who they are as people so that I can best help them learn." This leader was thrust into an ecotone she has been to many times. In fact, we all have been in these ecotones many times before. Yet, we seldom emerge with long-lasting solutions.

The coach decided to gently remove some people from the ecotone and work instead in that space with students willing to be trained, wanting to be successful, and willing to help others. By operating in this ecotone, isolated from the school ecosystem, the coach was able to excise those with unsurmountable values conflicts. The coach reflected, "The first thing I learned is the process of shifting mindsets is difficult; people have core values they believe in and will generally resort back to these." Additionally, she "also learned the importance of 'giving the work back' to the people who do the work as they implement something new. My teachers were more invested and felt more empowered when I used the ideas from the books we read as we developed and implemented professional development plans. Lastly, I learned that plans can and will change and change takes time."

This leader now knows how to use an ecotone she has been to many times before. She can now navigate more effectively and efficiently than she has in the past while simultaneously developing new relationships and strengthening existing ones.

Chapter 2

Understanding the Hacking Framework

Identifying challenges in life and work determines, in an essential way, whether we can actually ever change them. Our approach to solving challenges involves the amalgam of several frameworks from other practitioners and researchers, including Heifetz, Linsky, and Grashow's *The Practice of Adaptive Leadership* (2009), Garmston and Wellman's *The Adaptive School* (2016), Kegan and Lahey's *Immunity to Change* (2009), and Zoller's "The Philosophy of Communicative Intelligence in Cross-Cultural Collaboration" (2015). The amalgam is the result of combining elements from each of their frameworks to construct our own "Hacking Leadership Framework." The goals of hacking leadership are to more clearly identify a recurring and seemingly impermeable core challenge, work through a creative process, decide on an innovation, and try it out. Finding the hack and implementing it is what you do inside the ecotone.

In Figure 2.1, we start with "thinking" in order to create clarity about the challenge, its history, and the values involved. Then, if you realize the existing knowledge and values are not sufficient to solve the challenge, you can enter an ecotone. In the ecotone, you plan and create innovations (i.e., hacks) to test. Once you have devised the hack, you apply it and then monitor whether the challenge has been solved.

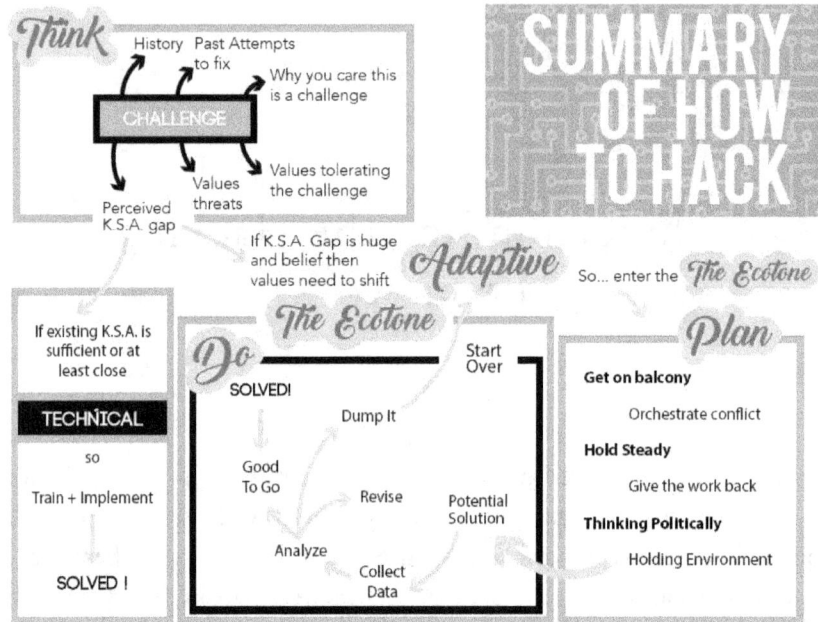

Figure 2.1: Part of any challenge is identifying the K.S.A. Gap: knowledge, skills, and abilities.

Now let us look more closely at the ecotone

Diving into an Ecotone

For all of us, challenges come and go. Some we look forward to, some we embrace, others we may dread, and the rest are somewhere in between. These challenges may be from work or home. For now, their source is not important. Oftentimes, we may try to ignore them. However, they are like smoke escaping from an open door; the challenge grows and permeates all available spaces in our lives. The enduring, nagging, festering challenges we experience are what can be termed "adaptive challenges" (Heifetz & Linsky, 2017).

When tackling an adaptive challenge, do some reconnaissance first. Identify the following:

1. Were you thrust into the challenge?

2. Do you find yourself returning to the same challenge with the same people and the same solutions?
3. Do you want to create a new space/place to do the work?

Remember the three main types of ecotones, used for simplicity and adaptive agility:

1. The ecotone you are *thrust into* because of an immediate circumstance: Perhaps while sitting in a meeting you realizing chaos is bubbling up and forcing instability. These instances can be accusations of project ineptitude, emerging time limitations, or internal conflict produced by the dynamics of those on the team. In any case, you are there, and you should take action.
2. The ecotone of places where you have *been before*: Perhaps you enjoy going there because they worked in the past and you navigated challenges successfully. Alternatively, they can be familiar places of chaos that did not work. The challenges here are not new; they just keep showing up as they have before.
3. The ecotone of your own choosing or creating: *You create* this ecotone because you see opportunities to move towards your destination. Leading from this ecotone is rewarding since you get to choose who comes with you, what you will bring, and how you will navigate it. This ecotone is like white water rafting. You are uncertain about what the ride will be like, but you have prepared yourself physically and mentally (see Figure 2.2).

All three ecotones have many things in common. There is chaos, there is unpredictability and instability, and often there are moving targets. Many people will experience discomfort, uneasiness, and trepidation here. All three ecotones require courage, resiliency, humility, and strong relationships. Inside the ecotone, as people collaborate around the "hack," they are also growing their relationships. These evolving relationships cause divergent thinking and a synergy where hacks emerge. People working together make the difference. What we know, what we can do, and how we feel are choices we make in the ecotones. The ecotone is the space to do work, to grapple with challenges in new ways, and to grow in the process.

Figure 2.2

From identifying the challenge to moving into the ecotone.

In our work with school leaders and leadership teams, we introduced adaptive leadership, immunity to change, communicative intelligence, adaptive schools, and the ecotone in order to work with their enduring, nagging, festering challenges. Using the words and experiences of school leaders, we will unpack these narratives and apply our thinking through the lens of the ecotone.

Using Table 2.1, we will extract pieces from the case studies. We will pose questions, challenge assumptions, and clarify the model. Our analysis intends to honor the incredible work of these urban school leaders while using their stories for other ways to approach these challenges. Many of the issues raised by these leaders are nagging, festering, and enduring challenges. Our hope is that their experiences can serve as a petri dish of innovation for us.

Table 2.1

Ecotone element	From the case study	Meditations on the ecotone balcony
The initial challenge		
Type of Ecotone		
What do I bring?	*Words from the cases study*	*Questions to drive thinking*
Whom do I bring?		
Values and beliefs		
ID the Ecotone Challenge		
Create and Innovate = The Hack		
Analysis — data and information		
Implementation and outcome		

The section below models the organization of the remainder of the book: a case study offered from real voices in the field. Each case study has a corresponding table with the ecotone elements and data from the case study, followed by our meditations from the ecotone balcony.

A Case Study Example

At a small pilot high school in one of the poorest, most marginalized communities in South Los Angeles, an instructional coach identified the adaptive challenge as the failure to complete assignments, and failure in classes. The coach's mantra for leading is *students first, content second.* The coach states, "I believe it is important to see my students for who they are as people so that I can best help them learn." This leader *was thrust* into an ecotone she has been to many times. In fact, we all have been in these ecotones many times before. Yet, we seldom emerge with enduring solutions.

The coach decided to gently remove some people from the ecotone and work instead with a group willing to be trained, wanting to be successful, and eager to help others. By having an ecotone, isolated from the rest of the school ecosystem, the coach was able to orchestrate a collision of values in a way that allowed her to excise those with unsurmountable conflicts. The coach reflected, "The first thing I learned is the process of shifting mindsets is difficult; people have core values they believe in and will generally resort back to these." Additionally, she "also learned the importance of 'giving the work back' to the people who do the work as they implement something new. My teachers were more invested and felt more empowered when I used the ideas from the books we read as we developed and implemented professional development plans and tracked our student progress. Lastly, I learned that plans can and will change and change takes time."

This leader now knows how to go to a new ecotone. She can now navigate more effectively and efficiently than she has in the past while simultaneously developing new relationships and strengthening existing ones (see Table 2.2).

Table 2.2

Ecotone element	From the case study	Meditations on the ecotone balcony
The initial challenge	Teachers kept failing students and this was not acceptable	Oftentimes, the thing we think of initially as a challenge is simply a symptom. It is data for us to use. In this case, the data was students failing. The deeper challenge is that teachers lacked sufficient knowledge and skills to address all students. When going to the ecotone, it is easier to have people with shared values, even though it may not always be possible. In the ecotone, this leader preserved and strengthened relationships. This is important because our relationships are the catalysts for the work. In the ecotone, consider a variety of hacks. Addressing challenges often requires a systems-thinking mindset. Operationalize the hacks, collect and analyze data, apply revisions, and then refine or discard.
Type of Ecotone	Been there before	
What do I bring?	New knowledge	
Whom do I bring?	Selected new team members	
Values and beliefs	- Success - Life-long learners - Collaboration	
ID the Ecotone Challenge	Teachers did not have the knowledge and skills to meet the needs of all students in their classes	
Create and Innovate = The Hack	- Collaboration to become more knowledgeable and create systems for students falling behind - New mindset	
Analysis — data and information	PD plans, data collection, and reflection	
Implementation and outcome	- Strengthened relationships - New relationships - Renewed common core values	

Chapter 3

Case Narratives

About the Case Studies

The 26 case narratives that follow are real stories and experiences from real practitioners in real schools. They are not perfect stories, as these people were just sharing their musings along the journey. They were written as reflective pieces as these educators worked to implement the models we had presented and they operationalized at their schools. The work of change is messy and the narratives are not sleek and simple. These are hard-working educators who leave out much of the triumph and despair that comes with the work.

In writing these narratives, these educators have reflected deeply on their own values and beliefs. They have identified a personal or institutional adaptive challenge and then moved into the ecotone to become a new kind of leader — an instructional leader. In doing so, they have also tried to master the Ecotone technique in order to tackle their adaptive challenges. Here is a quick reminder of the model.

Thinking
In working through these challenges, first identify what the challenge is and why it is important. The "what" of the challenge includes its history and past attempts to solve it. Second, identify the core values that drive the need to work on this challenge, which helps us see "why" this challenge is important. This facet also creates an environment where the values supporting the challenge are identified as well as the values threatened if the challenge continues. Clarifying those values supporting and those values threatened shows why the challenge is worth fighting.

One outcome of the thinking phase of the how-to-hack framework is identifying the knowledge, skill, and ability gap. This stage answers the question, "Are the existing Knowledge, Skills and Abilities (KSAs) sufficient to solve the challenge or is the gap sufficient enough to also warrant a shift in Beliefs and Values (BV)?" If the KSAs and BVs are to change, then the challenge is adaptive and we move to the planning stage at the edge of the ecotone.

Planning

The six practices and/or mindsets in this stage of hacking come from Heifetz and Linsky (2017). This stage continues to be a thinking-focused stage and it is the entrance into an ecotone. An ecotone, remember, is the place of tension between where the organization is and where you want it to go.

1. First, get on the balcony, which can be most easily summarized in one word: empathy. Metaphorically loom over the group, what do you see, hear, and feel? In what ways are you understanding from another's perspective? From the system's perspective?

2. Orchestrate conflict. When people have to change their values and beliefs as well as their knowledge, skills, and abilities, conflict will emerge. One key to successfully orchestrating conflict is to seek the level of disequilibrium significant to push people beyond their current capabilities to a level that is still within the limits of achievability. Not high enough to cause a shutdown, but still high enough to initiate change. We consider this to be the zone of proximal learning for adults.

3. Holding steady is about having clarity about what you believe and what you will do when you encounter conflicting values (within others or even within yourself). The messy work of leadership will inevitably butt heads with conflicting values.

4. Thinking politically is a pathway for building relationships and alliances with unlikely partners. It is about being willing to seek common ground with uncommon associations.

5. The holding environment is the crucible for conflict. In the holding environment you bring people who will engage in audacious honesty with moral vigor to test ideas and push thinking. The holding environment is where the hacks are made.

Doing

Once the plan is in place, we move to the "doing" stage. Here we fully enter the ecotone, the place for exploration — testing, data collection, and analysis — and revisions as necessary. In this place, refining is completed and then rolled out for implementation.

Cases

The cases below include samples from many different positions in education and are intended to help the reader understand how we define the ecotone and the amalgam of great frameworks we use to help schools grow. Ultimately, they serve as a platform for great people doing important work.

These case studies are intended for discussion, analysis, and debate and we have annotated them in three different ways in order to give the reader ideas about how to reflect on and explore the model: 1) text boxes, 2) editing tools, and 3) table format. At the end of this chapter you will also find a series of questions to deepen your understanding of the Ecotone model and to guide your group study and dialogue with colleagues. We hope you find these cases, their annotations, and the questions to be useful tools as we grow together.

We begin with two different adaptive challenges at the same school, one identified by the principal and one by the vice-principal (Cases 3.1 and 3.2). Next is an example of an educational leader who saw *himself* as the project requiring adaptation (Case 3.3). Later in the chapter, we include some charts (Tables 3.1 to 3.5) that can be used to help the reader analyze the key points of the case for reflection and discussion. Since these charts are useful for analysis, we have also included a blank one at the back of this book that can be copied and used for making notes on any of the cases or on your own hacking efforts.

Case 3.1: Principal

The School Context

Our school was founded in 2011 by a team of dedicated teachers seeking the autonomy to open an innovative, model arts school. As a part of the district's Public School of Choice reform measures, we were given the autonomy to innovate and offer a first-rate education in the arts. Our idea was that a rich immersion in the arts will teach students 21st-century skills, engage them in school, and lead to better outcomes in a struggling community. In 2014, the district acknowledged the growing demand our school was generating, and we converted to a magnet school, open to anyone living in the district's enrollment zone. We felt that our program was special enough that it needed to reach a wider audience. We are the first school in the city to be governed as an autonomous pilot school while enrolling as a magnet school.

Not satisfied with merely increasing outcomes, we committed to providing students with a college preparatory education combined with a world-class education in the arts. Students have access to a variety of arts programs including visual art, media arts, dance, drama, technical theatre, and music. In addition to and in concert with these thematic offerings, students have opportunities to take honors, advanced placement (AP), and college courses through a higher education campus on our school's campus during the regular school day. Our work is guided by our vision and we are a model of scholarship and arts education.

Students have infinite opportunities to grow and develop — their artistry, their academic achievements, and their abilities to become leaders in their communities. School graduates go to college prepared to succeed in any discipline, and embody our motto: Student, Citizen, Artist. Our school incorporates interdisciplinary teaching and arts integration to provide enriched learning for our students. Everyone is supplied with the technology and tools to be competitive against students of all backgrounds. The school provides in-depth, sequential arts programming that allows students to become accomplished artists. Expectations are high, we believe in second chances, our supports ensure success, and we celebrate achievements.

My Position

I was a co-founder, teaching colleague, and friend of the design team members when the school was first proposed. Our friendship and all we'd been through in our first years brought us closer for a time, but I've fou nd that as we continue, I'm not really seen as a friend anymore, but "the boss." That was hard for me to accept for a while, but once I accepted it, I managed to make the work less about personalities and more about job performance and group development. My personal objective is to ensure access to a rigorous academic and arts education for all children, and to model innovative leadership for school leaders nationwide. All of my work is done with an eye toward the future of transformative change in education and in people's lives. Key quotes I find inspirational and that help define me are these:

> *"Art itself is essentially ethical; because every true work of art must have a beauty or grandeur of some kind, and beauty and grandeur cannot be comprehended by the beholder except through the moral sentiment. The eye is only a witness; it is not a judge. The mind judges what the eye reports to it; therefore, whatever elevates the moral sentiment to the contemplation of beauty and grandeur is in itself ethical." — Edward G. Bulwer-Lytton*

> *"That which can be asserted without evidence, can be dismissed without evidence." — Christopher Hitchens*

> *"Education is what remains after one has forgotten what one has learned in school." — Albert Einstein*

The Adaptive Challenge

The adaptive challenge I have hacked and worked through focuses on our Election to Work Agreement (EWA). Since we opened our doors in 2011, our EWA is been reviewed and voted on each year. However, teachers did not seem to want to put in the time to really review the EWA and make changes. Mostly, I made suggestions that were accepted or not. A number of teachers would then complain throughout the year that they were being asked to do too much. They wanted to take PD days off or be paid for participating in essential events. Each year, I would remind everyone that this was their document — that they voted for it (not me), and yet I was expected to enforce it. Still, very little was done to make the changes they felt they wanted (or raised concerns about throughout the year). I assumed that when people are asked to do work that reflects their own best interests, and when they have near-complete control over it, that they would jump at the opportunity. I assumed that most remembered (except for new teachers, who often took it for granted) what the working conditions were like at their previous schools by comparison. Though we can make the conditions more difficult for one another with the expectations of the EWA, in fact, at our school, working conditions are considerably more teacher-friendly and supportive of their work. Many do not see it this way.

This was an issue driven by the Instructional Leadership Team (ILT), but it involved everyone from the faculty. In the fall of 2017, we were trying to determine what to focus on during the annual winter retreat in January 2018. Several ILT members and I felt that we needed to focus on a particular instructional issue at our school, based on the data we were looking at. Especially concerning to me was the implementation of Mastery Based Grading in a pilot group of teachers, none of whom were using the same grading system, which was confusing to students, to parents, and to me. This initiative was to be school wide in 2018–2019, but it had many problems, including an astronomical fail rate, leading many students to check out of school and jeopardizing many seniors' graduation prospects. However, the majority on the ILT were in favor of using the retreat time to do a thorough rewrite of the EWA, using input from the entire faculty, and going through a number of protocols to ensure that all voices were represented.

Ultimately, the majority on the ILT won out, and we decided to work on the EWA. I voiced my wish that, in order to maintain an instructional focus, we proceed with the understanding that we put students first in the rewrite, and create a document that upholds our vision and mission, not something that simply makes life easier. *We used a number of Adaptive Schools protocols to ensure an equal representation of voices in the ILT decision-making process, allowing one minute for advocating round robin, followed by discussion in which we reminded one another to practice pausing and paraphrasing as much as possible. Also, we used phrases such as "I'm going to put an idea on the table" and presented data as a third point. Personally, I did not want anyone to feel that my voice was outsized in the process (I can be pretty tenacious when I want to be, but tried to avoid that in this context).*

The key players in the ILT included the lead teacher (who has often been somewhat disgruntled), myself, a coordinator, two original design team members, and two new teachers. The lead teacher and the new teachers led the campaign for the EWA rewrite. After using the adaptive strategies to ensure that all voices were heard, we went through a final consensus strategy to arrive at an agreeable solution. Those who were not entirely bought in were asked what would move their vote from "I can't go along with it" to "I'll support it, even if I'm not crazy about it." This led us to choose the EWA work for our retreat. I do think that giving the teachers full autonomy over the EWA (which they always had but never embraced) caused the faculty to think more seriously about their reasons for teaching at a pilot school, and be more reflective of what they want to get out of teaching.

New Thinking and Outcomes

My relationships with teachers, especially those who were co-founders of the school, have changed quite a bit. While we are all cordial, I am no longer considered one of them, not invited to drinks or parties, and essentially no longer a friend to them. Given how immersive this career is, these were really my closest (and the majority) of my friends in the world. I had to grieve that loss over time, with about a year of being angry about it, followed by a year of sadness. *Now, I am in the acceptance phase, and do not take it personally, nor do I look to my colleagues for friends. The positive side is that I do not need to be conflicted when speaking to people about their performance or other issues that arise.*

In the process of stepping back from my own emotions and issues of control, even though they have helped us to be successful, I worry that I might lose a lot of my own voice in the school's growth. I am a bit worried too that I will lose my creativity in leadership of the school in favor of merely managing it according to the teachers' values. There is, however, universal acceptance of the EWA and more clarity about what is expected. One thing that recently came up is when one of the ILT members came to me wanting to be excused from our summer retreat (one of our requirements) for a learning opportunity. I ended up asking the teacher to present to the ILT, since the EWA is a teacher-to-teacher document, and any deviance from it (for a good reason or any reason) should be outlined to peers, not the principal. I have asked the ILT to make this the standing process.

The whole nature of leadership in this setting is one of balance: *How to maintain creativity, a personal vision, and a sense of freedom of ideas, while giving over leadership to others who may not have the same values. How can I be passionate while having to serve what might be the vision of others?* The truth is, I am not sure I can do it. I have always been most successful when given a large amount of leeway to pursue innovative and creative ideas, and when that is restricted, I feel like a manager and not really at my most effective. Because of this, it may be that "leading" a teacher-led school will not be the best fit for me. Time will tell.

Case 3.2:
Assistant Principal

The School Context
See Case 3.1.

My Position

I was one of the original design team members who helped write the plan and was a teacher in the first year of the school. As it became obvious that we would need an additional out-of-the-classroom staff member, I became a coordinator and then the assistant principal (AP). With only one AP and no coordinators, I wear many hats, so to speak. I am responsible for textbooks, EL programs, Title I, testing, the budget, the 1:1 iPad program, parents, teacher evaluations, discipline, compliance, etc. I love the range of duties and the contact with students, but it does feel overwhelming at times. I have also found that despite our efforts to be team-oriented and to share leadership, I am often expected to do anything but not have a voice. The Instructional Leadership Team (ILT) as a decision-making body is teacher-led, as it should be, but ends up making all the decisions that I then have to follow through on. I sometimes wish shared leadership went both ways. This might sound obvious, but I strive to give my best to all aspects of my work including problem solving a lost iPad, a student in distress, creating a schedule for testing, implementing instructional rounds — small tasks and larger projects, technical and adaptive challenges. I hope that I can be an administrator with integrity and a strong work ethic so I can inspire the same in others. My personal vision is shaped by several inspirational quotes such as these:

> *"A great man is always willing to be little."*
> *— Ralph Waldo Emerson*

> *"Convictions are more dangerous enemies of truths than lies." — Nietzsche*

> *"An opinion is a story robbed of its narrative."*
> *— Unknown*

The Adaptive Challenge

A challenge I undertook in my work focused on the new instructional schedule required. The schedule in place meant eight periods for each student, plus an advisory class. Teachers felt that their caseload was too large and students felt that they had too many classes to juggle. The students also felt — especially in their senior year — that they had too many non-essential classes. Two sides, represented by the arts department on the one side and by the math and English teachers on the ILT on the other, could not agree on what the schedule should be. One side argued from the perspective of sequenced arts classes, the other from the perspective of cross-curricular cohorts, advanced placement (AP) classes, and the like. *While there were obviously technical challenges related to the schedule, this tension made it clear that we were also dealing with conflicts among teacher values and beliefs, making this an adaptive challenge.*

I chose to address this issue because it felt closely tied to the core of what our school strives to be. *How do we juggle different academic and arts-related demands, all with an eye on what best addresses the needs and characteristics of our specific student population?* In the early stages of the discussion, we were looking over our past discussion notes and brainstorming ideas and it became obvious that one of the main sources of disagreement within the leadership team was which to prioritize — a rigorous academic program or a sequenced and robust arts program.

As this was the fourth schedule change in six years, I felt it was very important to consider how we had arrived at the current schedule so we would not go in circles and so we could revisit our reasons for deciding on past schedules, including how those served the needs of the different departments. I also insisted we make the counselor a part of the discussion as she had the clearest idea of the impact individual schedules have on the master schedule and which of our ideas were even realistic. The ILT put the schedule change on its agenda and I attended those meetings. For each meeting, everyone prepared ideas and questions to put on the table. I created a timeline to make sure we would have a decision made in time for the master schedule to be created. Ultimately, the faculty voted for one of the four schedules the ILT presented as options.

In ILT discussions, we used a variety of adaptive schools strategies to ensure that we would stay on task and have equal representation of voices. I used the "Ladder of Inference" as a way to remind myself, and others, to really hear other perspectives. I used charts to organize and visualize the group's thinking and to help the two sides better see the bigger picture. The key players in the ILT were the visual arts teacher and the instructional coach. Both were new to the school and unaware of the past schedule discussions we had. Additionally, we had a math teacher and the lead teacher. It seemed everyone wanted a new schedule and felt strongly that this would be the "fix" to all problems. On the other side were the principal, the coordinator, and myself, who felt that we needed to give the current schedule a few more years to be able to judge its effectiveness. The counselor was added to the discussion as an expert voice.

The schedule discussion really forced us to revisit our vision and mission. What does our school stand for? What do we believe is really best for our kids? What do we believe achievement means? *Each side felt they had the "right" values and that the other side's ideas would weaken these. Arguments were usually made along the lines of "If we want to be a _____ kind of school, then we must have _____, or else it's just empty words." We were able to find compromise in most cases. I think our willingness to let go of things for the greater good was a strength among us.*

Aside from a rift between arts and core teachers, there was a pronounced sense of distrust from the non-ILT staff towards the ILT. It took a lot of communication and clarity to ensure that all staff felt "in the know" and ready to vote at the end of the process. Relational trust was a bit low at times, but I believe it was strengthened at the end, as all faculty members voted and moved forward with a strong majority, ultimately feeling they had brought about change as a group. The tension that prevailed for a while showed everyone that we are no longer in the honeymoon phase of this school business. Things do not just flow and happen just because we are all passionate about education. There will be friction; we might not always agree; we might have to lose sometimes. These are all realizations we are beginning to make.

New Thinking and Outcomes

The immediate challenge has been resolved. There is a new schedule in place and everyone came to an agreement about it. The bigger challenge, however, will keep surfacing: how do we keep an open mind and really think through the issues the school faces rather than going to "fixes" like "we just need a new schedule" and then becoming blind in our advocating for what we believe is the way to go.

I think this might take another few years for us to figure out as a team. *The main lesson I learned, and continue to learn, is that in order to orchestrate conflict, I have to be emotionally distant.* I tend to see the school as "my baby," because so much of my life has gone into it as I continue to spend most of my time there. While that leads to a lot of dedication, it also makes me sensitive to change and criticism. So staying objective, looking at the big picture, hearing all voices, and staying focused on students are the strategies I need to use to be effective. I also learned that it is necessary sometimes to make people a bit uncomfortable in order to push their thinking, and make them aware of the biases and set perspectives. Ultimately, that leads to better collaboration and better results.

Case 3.3:
Assistant Principal

The School Context

As I reflect on our school's *vision*, I must consider the transformational journey and how it has brought me to this point of my own development as a school leader. Our vision states that we will prepare all students to be successful, viable members of an ever-changing global society. Our *mission* reflects our stakeholders' commitment to maintaining a nurturing learning environment in which teachers collaborate to develop rigorous, relevant learning opportunities for all students. As much as I wanted to focus on the positive changes in the culture and instructional outcomes that I have helped institute, or to pat myself on the back, the reality is that the most meaningful hacking I had to do in the past five years was to myself. From truly understanding coaching effective classroom instruction to defining what effective and meaningful student discipline is, I had to change my own dearly held previous mindset.

Values and Beliefs Not Matched by Behaviors

I always believed that we educate students "by any means necessary" without excuses no matter the challenge, setbacks, or obstacles, at any grade level or achievement gap in a student — "si se puede!" ("Yes, we can!"). This philosophy helped me push my students to be academically successful because of my belief that students will work to the level that we as educators demand of them. With that, I firmly believed that discipline had to be part of the education process because there was no time to waste. The fix was to see the problem, address student behavior, hand down consequences, and move on. I equated being stern with being fair and caring, not looking at the cause but only focusing on the outcome of student behavior and handing down punishment as the ultimate authority. Asking students "What is wrong?" and not "What has happened to you?" and receiving training in restorative practices (i.e., repairing broken relationships) changed that notion for me.

New Values and Beliefs

Students can be held accountable in a meaningful and supportive way that separates the student from the negative behavior and allows them to restore a broken relationship. *This led me to the ecotone to challenge how we too often superficially implement Maslow's theory of hierarchical needs by simply making it a check-off or a "to do" on our daily responsibilities as school leaders and educators.* Is what we are doing meaningful? How do we ensure that all school leader or stakeholder actions and program implementation fit into this pyramid to meet the needs of our students? Do students really trust us or feel safe and protected? Or are we implementing that "fake" caring from 8:30 am to 3:30 pm and then drive away from the community we serve?

How Did We Create and Innovate?
I hacked myself because I needed to be critical of the things that I was doing and actions I was talking as a school leader. *Being intentional and learning to use my professional voice to communicate the social and emotional needs of our students, their families, and the community was essential to me becoming not just better at my job, but better as a person.*

In the area of student learning and effective instructional practices, the dreaded reading list of books we sat through, listened to, and discussed on Saturday mornings in our ecotone professional development helped me find my instructional voice. This voice helped me to have meaningful, courageous conversations with my teachers about how to implement change and how to approach the craft of teaching, whether it be surface, deep, or transfer learning. Scripting lessons during classroom visits became the data and evidence to be analyzed, measured, and dissected to determine lesson effectiveness. In turn, teaching practices, content, and pedagogy was the focus of criticism, not the professional adult sitting next to me, which ultimately led to changes in classroom practice and the implementation of effective strategies to meet the learning needs of our students. As a result, feelings of being personally attacked began to disappear as classroom observation continued and a follow-up observation conference became the norm.

The Real Challenge
The biggest hack to my professional judgment on instruction was something that I was very familiar with but never quite knew how to verbalize: the development of positive teacher–student relationships in a classroom. Students will learn from a teacher and are willing to be held accountable when they know the teacher cares about them and their future, and believes that they will succeed against all odds. Again, this philosophy has always been part of my personal pedagogy. However, others outside of my classroom did not believe my students would or

could ever learn. Other educators — helpfully trying to make me feel okay with student failure — came up with various excuses. My students, they said, were only English learners, could not sit still, could not focus long enough to understand, or were attending an inner city school and therefore we should not expect much. These became reasons for me to prove these educators wrong. My students were not failures, and Hattie's work on meta-analysis of effective instructional practices[1] validated this by offering data that proved the importance of positive relationships in a school, ranking it higher than most instructional strategies. Essentially, we must first believe and care, and then teach.

Regarding my ability to deliver professional development, "The Adaptive School" philosophy led to growth in my mindset. All meetings now begin with expected meeting norms and explicit meeting objectives, with tangible teacher work produced at the conclusion of every meeting. Implementing timelines and team member responsibilities are the norm. Now team members hold each other accountable instead of me doing it. In turn, we believe it is not just my responsibility, but the responsibility of all of us to ensure student success.

New Thinking and Outcomes

In order to arrive at this point of my leadership development, the hacking had to happen in me. I needed to find a space and a place to embrace my own development. Hacking myself in this ecotone before hacking the systemic low student academic expectations was critical. This led me to curb superficial caring and ticking off boxes to demonstrate that something was done. We eventually found ourselves moving away from quantity to quality, from meaningless professional discussions on pedagogical practices to what needs to change to ensure student success. To this end, I have realized that it is me who needs to continue to grow and "hack" my beliefs so that others will trust my leadership and understand the importance of a "we" and not a "me" culture. The "we" culture will bring the changes needed to move our school forward. I can learn from team members just as much as they can learn from me. Behaviors and practices

---

1 See John Hattie's various publications on "visible learning."

can change. Change is a process and not a product. Ultimately, I can trust in my own leadership abilities and know my worth and the worth of all others.

Case 3.4: Assistant Principal Secondary Counseling Services

The School Context

The school I work at is the oldest public high school in this large urban school district. Established in 1873, it celebrated 100 years in its new location. The school is predominantly Latino (79%), with about 10% African American, 5% Asian American, 3% Filipino, and 2% Caucasian. This school has experienced much transition over the last ten years, including restructuring, loss of instructional staff, reduced funding, and changed administrative staff. Our mission promotes a dynamic learning community that fosters empathy, creativity, critical thinking, effective communication, and collaboration. The school's vision focuses on a commitment to ensure that all students graduate with the skills they need to build lives of personal satisfaction, responsibility, and success.

Social justice has come to the school in bulletins and mandates that encouraged us to reduce the number of student suspensions. We are now, therefore, using community circles organized in the restorative justice framework in lieu of suspensions. Socio-emotional counseling is overseen on campus by mental health partners and by the school psychologist.

I am the Assistant Principal Secondary Counseling Services. The biggest task in my position is to create and maintain a master schedule of classes aligned with the district and state A–G standards. I also supervise three academic counselors, one college counselor, one PSA diploma counselor, and one attendance counselor. However, other duties include senior class activities, graduation, articulation, monitoring and maintaining the student support and progress team, evaluating instructional staff, creating and implementing professional development workshops, monitoring and maintaining student grades and credit recovery programs, and networking with parents and community members, specifically announcing open houses and parent conferences.

My personal vision for my work is to engage the staff in a professional learning community model facilitating the discovery and implementation of instructional strategies that efficiently prepare students for college and career readiness. A few quotes that define who I am include the following:

> *"One mind, one vision preparing our students for college and career." — Unknown*
>
> *"When teachers teach, students learn." — Unknown*
>
> *"If you never give up, you will never fail." — Unknown*

The Adaptive Challenge

My challenge is to find ways of providing feedback that help teachers grow. This is an adaptive challenge in a district where a strong teachers' union tells members to not cooperate or listen to administrators.

I chose to focus on "scripting" for teacher feedback. Although scripting was easy for me — recording the time, the number of students, what the teacher said, what the student said, how many students were in the classroom, etc. — providing positive instructional feedback presented a challenge. It is a personal challenge, one revolving around my desire to be accepted and, if not accepted, at least valued and obeyed. I believe this is the wrong attitude and that acceptance and

> **Competing areas of importance is one source of tension, such as getting information that can improve instruction back to teachers. The other is supporting a union that fights for the rights of teachers. The challenge here is not finding ways of providing feedback, which has an easily implemented technical fix. The deeper challenge has to do with the school culture and the relationship between faculty and administration.**

respect are earned over time once trust is built. Building trust requires repeated success, where staff can see the benefits of a particular strategy practiced and expanded with even more success. I believe that honoring my true self and the strategies that I have successfully used in the past will need to be modeled to my peers in this new position. Repeat successes will attract interest from some; however, I also acknowledge that others will never adapt. I will identify and work with people who are willing to change from their old ways of thinking and behaving that no longer yield productivity. Essentially, I must maintain efficient and ethical principles in a hostile work environment. I must not lose my focus, take attacks personally, or act unprofessionally. Working together, we will build a school that moves students and teachers to success.

I chose this challenge because I believe in the sincerity of the teacher. I believe that most educators want to help students. One of the Student Success and Progress Team (SSPT) norms is "remember this is a democracy, not a dictatorship," and everybody's voice must be heard. Actively listening to, and respecting the voices of others opens the door for new ideas to flourish that can help the school grow and accomplish its mission. The personnel involved in my adaptive challenge were the counselors, teachers, and staff. First, I made a commitment to respect the voices of others. Second, I practiced flexibility and loyalty to the ideas of others even when I did not agree with them. Third, I invested time and talent to demonstrate my commitment to the group process. Fourth, I did not give up. I am still at the beginning stages and I am seeing some positive results. Counselors and teachers visit my office and share their successes and challenges. Staff stand with me during stressful situations and we work together to maintain focus. We are moving forward.

New Thinking and Outcomes

My principal shared his vision and mission with me. My counselors shared their challenges and hopes with me. Teachers shared their frustrations and wish lists with me. I responded supportively, making mental and visual notes. My

I created a personal ecotone to develop my skills for listening and developing empathy and creating a culture of collaboration.

decisions and actions are aligned with the vision, mission, hopes, and wish lists shared with me. I used data including surveys, the teaching and learning framework, the districts counselor job duties, recommendations from my mentor, and team building activities, as well as research based strategies shared at workshops.

I continue to be amazed at the power of the group. My relationships with certain counselors and out-of-classroom staff were challenged. However, I believe that my relationships with most were strengthened. I also believe that my relationship with students, teachers, parents, and my principal were strengthened. I gave up my time and I would do it again because it leads to positive gains for the students and to solidifying relationships. I learned that having an open mind and doing what works pays off. But not everyone will travel the road with me and when I feel like I'm travelling alone it is only because I cannot see what is ahead of me and I do not look behind me.

Case 3.5: Assistant Principal

The School Context

Ours is a charter school opened in 2002 with one class of students and now expanded to nearly 600 students. It began as a school that served the local community made up of educated, upper-middle-class working professionals. Over the years, the student demographic has changed. The school is now comprised of a wide variety of students, most of whom are considered "at-risk," growing up in poor and devastating conditions. The increased number of students and the shifted student demographic is reflected in the school's test scores. The school has done a great job of developing the school culture and fostering a sense of family and community on campus. However, the data shows a lot of room for growth regarding academics.

As the Assistant Principal of Curriculum and Instruction, much of my responsibility entails developing effective teachers. I co-plan with teachers, observe their lessons, co-teach, and provide feedback and coaching. I evaluate the current curriculum and how to enhance it. I am also responsible for the school's professional development. Research proves that the effectiveness of the teacher has the largest impact on student achievement and learning. Therefore, it is my duty to ensure that teachers are as effective as possible for the good of our students. We need to prepare students to be successful in their futures. This means that teachers need to be prepared to be successful in their classrooms. My job is to help them with that. Here are two of the numerous quotes that inspire me:

"When you learn, teach, when you get, give."
— Maya Angelou

"Not all of us can do great things. But we can do small things with great love." — Mother Theresa

The Adaptive Challenge

Finding and developing skilled teachers who can meet the needs of diverse learners is an adaptive challenge.

One adaptive challenge I chose to hack in my school dealt with a struggling and challenging male teacher. The issue with this teacher was that there was very little effective teaching actually happening in the classroom.

As you think about this problem, what emerges for you as the adaptive issue? The teacher's skill of teaching, classroom management, lesson planning? What do you think this teacher's values are?

This challenge is process focused — i.e., how do we find and develop good teachers... The teachers they have do not possess the skills, knowledge, or abilities to meet the needs of their students. If they found teachers with these skills, would this solve the issue explained below?

This teacher taught an art class focusing on technology. When I would walk into his classroom, there would be about seven of his

30 students working on the content and engaged in the learning process while the others did whatever they wanted on the computers. His room was often dark with films playing as students worked. It was filled with students ditching other classes, and there were always students on their phones and eating and drinking. The room was always dirty and smelled bad. This teacher would not turn in lesson plans or unit plans. Whenever we had professional development or a staff meeting about new instructional strategies or school rules and protocols, he was the first to say why the new idea would not work or did not make sense. The biggest issue of all was the fact that his class was not serving as a good use of instructional time for our students. Neither their minds nor their spirits were nourished.

As the administrator trying to coach this teacher, I would spend several hours a week trying to work with him and figure out an approach that met both of our needs. We discussed unit planning at length and he expressed that using traditional planning templates did not work for him because he saw things in a visual, abstract way. I encouraged him to create unit plans through a storyboard design instead to help him express himself artistically. He would agree and I would spend time developing these plans with him. Still, he would never finish or would not use the plans in the classroom. I figured out we needed to start smaller. But we would make some progress, and then he would revert to his old ways. I was spending a great deal of my time with very few results.

I chose this challenge because it caused me quite a bit of frustration. I could feel myself becoming discouraged, which I did not like. I knew I had to come up with better solutions for the good of the students.

The author states that "the good of the students" is an important value. What other important value clashes with that of the good of the students?

I also knew that I would not be able to solve this challenge alone. Those involved in this process were my principal, the teacher, a teacher leader, the Charter Management Organization's (CMO) director of art, and myself. When I saw that my approach was not working well with this teacher, I met with the 12th grade teacher leader and our principal. We discussed our concerns with this teacher and the approach that had been taken thus far. Our teacher leader was willing to provide support for this teacher. We determined when he would observe and co-plan. We also put the teacher on an improvement plan so that our expectations were clear. The teacher had the choice of sharing that plan with his teacher leader, which he did. We also used the support of the Director of Art of the CMO. We expressed our concerns and gave her one specific area in which she could help.

New Thinking and Outcomes

The overall experience showed me how much accountability, trust, and dedication to our students all mean to me. Throughout the Charter and Autonomous School Leadership Academy (CASLA) program at CSU Dominguez Hills, we learned how effective, hardworking teachers can be turned off from the profession because of other teachers not being held accountable on campus. That is something that stuck with me and accountability became an important value. This challenge strengthened that because many of our strong teachers were feeling more and more frustrated by the fact that enforcing school rules and professional norms had to be discussed at each PD when everyone knew it was the same handful of teachers ignoring the expectations. I made it a point to stop having these discussions with the whole group and start holding individuals accountable.

My relationship with this art teacher was challenging in many ways. However, the more I learned how to communicate and be transparent with the teacher, the more it actually improved. The art teacher felt he could trust me and felt comfortable expressing himself. My relationship with our teacher leader was also strengthened by the experience. He felt empowered by the experience and really stepped up as a leader. I felt proud to help build capacity in one of our strongest teachers. I also learned how to give up some control. When I saw the way our teacher leader was able to step in with much more success, it encouraged me to allow others to take on more responsibility in other areas. I had been putting a lot of pressure on myself and I struggled with delegating at times.

This challenge helped me to strengthen my ability to build capacity in others and trust the process.

> Tensions emerge when values clash. This assistant principal values putting students first. They also value putting relationships with the adults on campus first by building trust and respecting autonomy, which creates a clash in their personal ecotone. As you think about tensions between your own values, what are some ways you can address and resolve them?

Although the art teacher has made a bit of growth and is working on planning, not enough progress has been made. We are all still working to support the teacher, but it is becoming more and more evident that our school may not be the best fit. We are preparing to have that conversation. As a result of the ecotone, I learned the importance of collaboration, of delegation, of trusting in strong team members, and of knowing when it is time to cut ties for the good of the students.

Case 3.6: Instructional Leadership Team

The School Context

Ours is a small charter high school founded in 2011. Our student population of 350 is over 90% Hispanic/Latino and about 98% of the students qualify for free or reduced lunch. Regarding social justice and mission, our challenge is to provide our scholars with the tools necessary to be successful after graduation. After analyzing the school's biggest gaps and needs, we have transitioned our focus to developing strategic literacy instructional practices among all teachers with relevant pedagogy and content. Because of this transition, our school has developed an Instructional Leadership Team (ILT) with the chairs of ELA, math, and science along with the principal. In addition to our transition in focus, our school is also dealing with the challenge of under-enrollment, which has meant budget cuts, leaving us with only one administrator on campus, the principal. This lack of administration has forced our teachers to step up and take on administrative roles such as conducting PDs around literacy strategies and evaluation rubrics that will best support the needs of our scholars, as well as feedback on lesson plans and unit plans, informal classroom observation, and Beginning Teacher Support and Assessment (BTSA) induction assistance.

I began my teaching career at this school — a memorable year filled with learning experiences. In its second year of service, the school lost its principal along with 90% of the staff. I remember being just as lost as all the other teachers, given that about 70% of the new hires were in their first year of teaching. In my department, I was one of three new teachers who took on the role of teaching mathematics. Our department chair taught upper level followed by the middle group in Geometry. I took on the freshman with Algebra 1 and Support along with one Pre-Calculus section. With three brand new courses, I definitely had some late nights. It was an extremely challenging year, not only with my scholars, but with the administration. The principal was absent most of the time due to pregnancy. The assistant principal, displaced from his last school due to unprofessional behavior, managed in the principal's absence. This unstable situation led to discrepancies that had to be dealt with by human resources. Nevertheless, I survived, and learned so much, not just in my classroom teaching but also how to deal with difficult adults. During my second year at the school, we lost our department chair and eventually lost our second teacher.

In light of this transition, I decided to step up and spoke my principal about taking on the department chair role and opening up a section for AP Calculus AB and eventually AP Calculus BC. I knew that we had scholars ready for more mathematics and equipped with the knowledge and skills to perform at the college level. In my third year of teaching, my scholars and I were able to attain a 100% pass rate in AP Calculus BC. I developed a special feeling for the higher levels of mathematics and lost focus on those not performing at this level. Many of our scholars are not fortunate enough to make it to this level, so I knew I had to reflect on how I could better support the larger population in their mathematics endeavors.

This year, I have taken on Pre-Calculus, AP Calculus, and IM3, the junior year mathematics course that all of our scholars must pass in order to graduate and prepare for the California Assessment of Student Performance and Progress (CAASPP). In teaching this course, I have been able to reflect on and understand the areas of growth and the gaps our scholars have regarding content knowledge and the skills necessary to perform well in their math class and on CAASPP. I was able to appreciate all the hard work of our teachers and reflect on my role as department chair and my new role of instructional leader for the math teachers. In this new role, I have noticed a tremendous shift in terms of the literacy demands of mathematics, which are sky high. The problems our scholars face on the CAASPP exam require advanced reading skills in order to figure out what it is they need to solve. The creative thinking process required also needs to be practiced every day of classroom instruction.

To improve our performance, I provide feedback on lesson plans, unit plans, and with informal observations. I also work with our ILT to provide meaningful professional development around best practices for literacy strategies and GROW (Teacher Evaluation Rubric). Additionally, it is my job to support our math teachers in developing workable literacy strategies. As the instructional leader for mathematics, I have been conducting data meetings where our teachers sit down, analyze, and discuss student work and performance. They focus on identifying misconceptions and finding creative methods to address them.

The Adaptive Challenge

The adaptive challenge I hacked involved a transition process. In my work as an ILT, I am faced with transitioning from being a classroom teacher to being a coach. In my department, I have two additional teachers and I also oversee the Spanish department.

One adaptive challenge is simply moving from the teacher role to the coaching role.

Most of the teachers I work with are very receptive and open to feedback and change. In particular, I co-teach IM3 with my IM2 (sophomore teacher), who has been very open to feedback and even allows me to film our coaching conversations. However, the same cannot be said of my IM1 teacher, with whom I co-teach Pre-Calculus. My IM1 teacher, is not very open to my feedback (because I am not officially administration and because she has taught for the same number of years as me) and misses quite a few work days due to illness. For example, she did not show up for our first two data meetings.

I chose this challenge because I know how frustrating this situation is for both of us and I know that these types of challenges will definitely arise in future. Being able to exercise flexibility and empathy are skills that I know I need to work on. In my transition from teacher to administrator, I want to be able to work around the challenges while remaining caring and understanding of my team's own challenges.

This coach discovered that when coaching, you are talking about someone's profession. Since we can't control how someone receives a message, we must try to control how we give feedback and express empathy.

In this challenge, my team (specifically my IM1 teacher), my principal, and I are involved. We are in a good place right now. After making several adjustments to our working relationship and reflecting on my communication with my team and the principal, I believe the challenge was addressed to the best of my ability. Looking back, I understand now that I was taking this challenge too personally. In my role as instructional leader, I need to lead by giving the work back to my team. Communicating the importance of the work is essential.

When the first data meeting was missed, I made sure I had everything set up in our team drive. I constructed the folder with the necessary data and Data-Driven Instruction (DDI) tool for all my teachers to analyze their scholar performance and misconceptions. I emailed the IM1 teacher, letting her know that I hoped everything was okay and attaching the links for the DDI tool and data to help her complete her action plan and analysis. The following day, I trained her on how to access the results for her scholars on our new testing software, Illuminate.com. Then I gave her the deadlines and let her know I was available if she needed any further assistance.

When the second data meeting was missed, I followed the same process to make sure that the expectations were communicated. After interim 2, the results in scholar growth were evident so I was sure we were on the right track. After interim 3, I noticed a decline in her scholar achievement. I spoke to my principal about my concern that her decline in scholar performance directly correlated with her excessive absences. My principal shared that the IM1 teacher was suffering from diabetic flare ups and was covered under the Family Medical Leave Act (FMLA), which meant that there is nothing we can do on our end but support her.

I communicated to my other teachers about the excused absences and made sure we were all focused on moving our academic achievement forward. In working through this challenge, I leveraged the team drive and Gmail to make sure that expectations and resources were shared and always available. And I did manage to grow my empathy and flexibility. Eventually my IM1 teacher was able to trust me enough to tell me herself about her diabetes and the reason behind her absences.

New Thinking and Outcomes

Going into this work, I had no idea that it would help me build stronger relations with my team. Expressing empathy was definitely one of my weaknesses and I knew I had to own that. Checking in on a regular basis, stopping by classrooms, sending appreciative notes, asking for help myself (showing vulnerability), and going out for lunch on our data days are all strategies that helped me work more effectively with my team. Teachers

As you think about this adaptive challenge, will mastery to communicate with flexibility and empathy resolve this coach's challenge? Perhaps the adaptive challenge is something quite different. Come up with three or four challenges for this coach (besides knowledge and skill) that include shifts in values and beliefs about their role as a coach. You may want to include an explanation about how the current school culture may support or conflict with the adaptive challenge.

are human beings and part of the work is being human with each other. At the end of the day, it is not about us, it is about our scholars. They deserve a team who can work together regardless of our differences to help them improve their academic achievement.

As you think about this adaptive challenge, will mastery to communicate with flexibility and empathy resolve this coach's challenge? Perhaps the adaptive challenge is something quite different. Come up with three or four challenges for this coach (besides knowledge and skill) that include shifts in values and beliefs about their role as a coach. You may want to include an explanation about how the current school culture may support or conflict with the adaptive challenge.

In a way, I gave up a little control but I also gave up my fear of coaching other teachers. I can now reflect on this experience and use the lessons learned for my teaching and administrative years to come. The challenge was resolved adaptively. Being able to work around differences is key to maintaining the good relationships essential for the hard work to get done. Through this challenge, I learned what it means to be a collaborative leader by being empathetic towards my team. My weakness has always been expressing empathy. I never understood why, but now I know it is because I was so concentrated on myself and on my own classroom. In a way, I felt that I should not have to feel sorry for anybody. I felt that if I worked hard, others should also be working hard. I have always been very independent and never afraid to figure things out on my own. This challenge helped me become more of a team player and willing to work with other teachers. Today, I have a new definition of a leader: one who empathizes and is caring for others. This model will help me motivate teachers and impact the achievement of all our scholars. It is our students who feel the impact of our teamwork the most.

Case 3.7:
Pupil Services and Attendance Counselor (PSA)

The School Context

Our high school is comprised of 70% male and 30% female students. We have 94% Hispanic students, 4.7% African American, 0.2% American Indian, and 1.2% white. In my three years at the school, I have noticed that racial tension between our Hispanic and African American population has lowered because our wonderful principal wanted to be more inclusive. He added African American staff, alleviated racial issues, built relationship and community, and educated students about cultural biases.

We strive to educate our students around cultural biases and encourage them to be socially responsible. Our mission is to prepare our students with strong foundations in reading, writing, mathematics, critical thinking, and problem solving skills using creative digital and media literacy. Although we are constantly revisiting instructional strategies and practices, our administration ensures that teachers are provided with the support they need. We always put student learning and student needs first. Our vision for our students is three-fold: 1) succeeding for today through the cooperative involvement of students, parents, educators, and the community; 2) preparing for tomorrow via technology, focusing on academic achievement, and a college-going culture; and 3) learning for a lifetime to become productive citizens.

I currently serve as the attendance counselor and am responsible for pupil services. The focal point of my duties is to ensure that students are attending, are engaged, and are on track towards graduation. I provide mental health counseling and assessments as needed, educating students and parents around education codes and the law around attendance. I provide students with academic guidance and community resources that will help remove barriers to regular attendance. I conduct home visits, parent meetings, student groups, and present student cases at the district attorney's office. Aside from my regular responsibilities, I also provide incentives to students who are meeting our attendance goal, provide data to all stakeholders around our attendance, organize school-wide assemblies, and lead the School-Wide Positive Behavior Intervention support committee. Additionally, I serve as a liaison for our youth who are homeless or in foster care.

My personal vision for my work stems from my belief that my time is precious, our time here on earth is finite, and I must use it wisely. How I do my job and live my life determines what will become of me after death. I learned that I must do whatever it takes while going through the administrative credential program. At times lose track of what our calling is on this earth. We put aside what it is important: family, life, love, empathy, etc. I sometimes berate myself for not having the data that the district asks of me. But when I reflect on all that I have done for my students, I am still doing more than what is expected of me. I am doing whatever it takes to get their basic needs met. I am going above and beyond to ensure that they feel cared for and loved so that they eventually show up at school. I feel that this counts so much more than the data. My relationships with my students have so much meaning and value. Their education will eventually show that and I will know how much of a difference I have made on that student.

The Adaptive Challenge

The adaptive challenge I hacked focuses on my various responsibilities. As a PSA counselor, you are trained to ensure that students are attending school, engaged, and on track to graduate. But your trainers never tell you how challenging it can be. When I arrived at our school, teachers were used to doing things their own way because there was little to no accountability for monitoring attendance. Our current principal wanted to change this and trusted me to help with the process. Aside from ensuring that students show up, I also have to ensure that attendance is taken correctly for auditing purposes. I cannot even begin to describe how much pushback I received from the teachers because I "was telling them what to do." I have to admit that I did not take the time to look at the vision of the

The autonomy theme rears its head. This counselor discovered how highly teachers value autonomy — sometimes over everything else.

school, to investigate the culture, and to build relationships. It was a challenging year.

I felt defeated at times, that I was doing something wrong. I had conversations with my principal about the challenges and the pushback I was receiving from teachers. I thought that maybe he could send an email or tell them that they were not doing their job. I was wrong. A colleague and friend of mine introduced me to the book *Leadership on the Line*. After reading it, I understood that I had to "get on the balcony" and check the temperature of the school. Aside from that, I started to get involved in School-Coordinating Council (SSC), Instructional Leadership Team (ILT), and School-Wide Positive Behavioral Interventions and Supports (SWPBIS). I needed to be more visible and involved by learning about our school's vision and culture, and begin to build relationships of my own. I asked our union representative what the union says about attendance taking. I began to recognize teachers who were submitting their attendance forms 100% of the time on a monthly and weekly basis. I began to create challenges and raffle gift cards. It amazed me how competitive teachers were becoming. Yet, that was not enough. I felt that I was still missing a piece of the whole puzzle.

In my third year at the school, I decided to go back to school and join a local school leadership program. It has been the best decision I have ever made. It has opened the door for continuous learning. I understood the work of teachers and felt the need to support them more so than ever. I started by asking to sit in for classroom observations and really experiencing what it is like to be in the classroom. As part of my field project, I decided to be more transparent in the work that I do as a PSA so that teachers would also understand what I was doing. I wanted them to know why I do what I do. I started to share data around attendance and attendance submittal. I also began to share the amount of funding we were losing per day because attendance was not being submitted and students were not being accounted for. This helped shift teacher behavior so that attendance became part of their vision too.

This can be viewed as a personal ecotone as well as one chosen to go into collaboratively with teachers.

Despite the many systems to put in place, I felt that we had accomplished so much. I had to look within myself, bring out my leadership skills, and put them to work.

I had to shift my mindset and not think about what is not being done but how we were going to do it as a team. I began to give the work back and at the same time I also put myself into our teachers' shoes to think of how to make their jobs simpler and not add to their plate. I feel that I am slowly getting there and having more courageous conversations around why and how I will help support them in their classrooms. I chose this challenge because I had to change my thinking before I began doing the work. I cannot be more thankful to my friend who had a courageous conversation with me about this challenge and handed me that book. It has transformed my leadership and I have been able to apply all the tools in any setting I am in.

I felt that I needed to reach out to the strongest teachers in the school first because they would help me understand the teacher's challenges. In addition, I reached out to our support staff. They have helped me challenge myself around presenting to all stakeholders and being transparent. I also have to say that the tools I learned in the school leadership program has helped me to shift my mindset to the type of leader I aspire to be.

This counselor saw the power of influence in relationships and in having a culture of collaboration.

New Thinking and Outcomes

My value of privacy was a challenge for me. I was raised thinking that one should keep things private, especially negatives ones, not expose them. I was doing a lot of good work and not being transparent about it. In terms of our attendance data, I have learned that it is not within my control that students live with trauma in a low socioeconomic community and that gangs and drugs continue to be large issues. What I do have control over are the relationships and connections I make with them in helping them cope with that trauma. Once I challenged myself to share the work I was doing, teachers had more respect for it (and me) and were more willing to collaborate. I was also challenged to get out of my comfort zone. If I want to be a leader, I need to be willing to be vulnerable and share the truth about our attendance data, regardless of how bad it looks. My negative mind set of "it can't be done" has shifted to "how can it be done?" I have to be willing to think outside the box, get on the balcony, and give the work back. We are all in education for what is best for our students.

I was also able to build relationships in the least expected places, with teachers who did not believe in me or in the work that I did, with teachers who were not welcoming when I first arrived. I had to challenge myself to work with them, and now we collaborate so much more than before. I still feel some pushback, but I will do whatever it takes to get the work done for our students.

I did lose my negative thinking that things would not change and teachers do not care. They just have a lot of pressure, so I need to support them as much as they need to support me. I also had to give up putting myself down for not pushing the attendance up to where it should be. Although this data is important, students themselves are the priority.

Our school is in continuous growth mode because we do have many new teachers. I am proud to say that we have now put systems in place. They are not perfect but it is refreshing to know that you can always improve them. I am having more courageous conversations with our teachers around attendance, instruction, and support in the classrooms. As educators, we have to do whatever it takes to ensure that our students are learning, graduating, and moving on to college. Being a leader is challenging. There is no one size that fits all. I have to remain a constant lifelong learner and ensure that I model that for those that I am leading.

> **This case is another example of an ecotone that shifted from its original form. What began as a need to develop professional roles shifted to changing mindsets and how to approach relationships.**

Case 3.8:
Assistant Principal

The School Context

Our school is co-located with three other schools. There has been declining enrollment for the last few years and gradually we are faced with challenges that are beyond our control. Our organization's mission and vision has been to create schools that are going to serve the most vulnerable students. Its mission has been to provide students with opportunities to achieve their best and take advantage of educational programs that will prepare them for college. Our student population is 95% Latino and 85% of the student population is on free and reduced lunch. Our school has gone through many changes in the last few years as the leadership team took part in the Innovative School Leadership Institute (ISLI) team. We dedicated a lot of time to sharpen our instructional focus. Literacy is the core of all our efforts in writing the new vision and mission statement.

We successfully implemented a school-wide focus on checking for understanding so we already had this experience of taking a hack and making it work. Identified a former hack to use as a touchstone for the new work.

The school itself has transformed through the years as we have implemented many changes.

I have been an Assistant Principal for few years now with a variety of duties and responsibilities. I am an instructional leader first and foremost. I also oversee special education and student services. I do a lot of work with families in ensuring they are connected to necessary resources such as mental health and other counseling needs.

My vision for my work is to be an advocate for our students and, at the same time, be an advocate for the teachers. As a school leader, I believe it is critical to be able to balance these two in approaching situations of conflict or change. Bolman and Deal's (2017) framework has been a good foundation for me as I transitioned from the classroom to school leadership, helping me conceptualize many of the approaches that I can take in different circumstances. *The Practice of Adaptive Leadership*

(Heifetz, Linsky, & Grashow, 2009) has also been a valuable resource for me, especially in schools that need organizational change. Learning how to adapt is essential in responding the right way so that you can build trust but at the same time have those brave and honest conversations.

As an assistant principal, my role has been to support the principal with her vision and share the burden of leading the school through effective research-based practices. It has taken me some time to prioritize my roles and define my purpose. As *Adaptive Leadership* states, "your purpose helps you allocate your time and how you furthered your purpose each day." I have created systems and put structures in place for my own work and responsibilities and have prioritized my duties so that I can be clearer with my purpose and goals.

The Adaptive Challenge

We have seen an immense need for discipline overhaul because teachers felt that they were not being supported by the administration when it came to discipline. Resentment from the teachers and staff built up because some of them did not believe that discipline was being handled the way it needed to be. Part of the issue was that there was no transparency and clarity around discipline policies and how issues were being addressed by the administration. I chose this challenge because it has really framed my leadership lens in the effort it took as a school to really become adaptive and transparent. This is still an ongoing challenge because we are still in the process of establishing school-wide practices and staying true to the policies we know will be effective.

> This adaptive challenge seems to be a common one at many schools. How do we meet the needs of students and help them be successful at school academically and behaviorally? The need to overhaul the system is a solution and a great example of how it takes time to get to the real diagnosis.

Most stakeholders were involved in the process of implementing restorative practices to address the discipline concerns of the teachers. At the same time, we needed to use that practice in addressing the accountability placed on us by the district in terms of achieving a 0% suspension rate. The initial conversations began organically as more and more teachers started speaking out, providing their honest reflections. The instructional leadership team decided that we needed to reflect on these issues as a school in order to decide how to move forward in establishing safety for students and support for teachers. We were introduced to restorative practices and we knew that it would be worthwhile to explore them given how some schools had transformed when they had implemented this practice. We began by getting more training and attending seminars on restorative practices so that the leadership team would be able to educate the staff.

This group went to a new place for their ecotone.

First, we really did have to get up on the balcony and look at the overall picture and we used the steps of "How to Hack" to be effective and get real results. As we received more training, we introduced the concept and how to roll it out, first with individual teachers and then on a school-wide basis. We used several professional development meetings to introduce restorative practices and addressed any concerns from teachers. We met as a team to figure out what to do when students misbehave in the classroom and how to be proactive, rather than reactive, in addressing those concerns ahead of time.

All the valuable seminars we took about trauma informed our practices. We actually took that Adverse Childhood Experience (ACE) Questionnaire (n.d.) as a staff to better understand our own traumas. This was really a mind-opening experience because everyone reflected on their own results and started thinking about how our students would score on this survey. It was a good starting point because staff members realized that our students are very vulnerable and need us to understand that. We discussed our plan in a community circle once a week. The students were involved in the process as well because they had to know the "why" of community circles. The classified staff also had to buy into this adaptive challenge. We wanted everyone's behavior to reflect what we were trying to achieve so we had to be really clear about the expectations and outcomes. We wanted students and staff to feel part of our community and to help build that community in order to use restorative practices.

We utilized the team as a whole and relied on their expertise and training, using many of the tools from our restorative practices training, including the ACE survey. Forming circles during advisory periods was critical in building community in each classroom. We used the essential elements of restorative practices to address discipline issues as they were brought to our attention. We decided on the tools needed to collect the data required to truly reflect on this new initiative.

We had to challenge the staff to be honest and vulnerable during this process. We had to really trust each other to be able to share our own interests/views based on our backgrounds/experiences. The staff really grew closer because we would start meetings doing a circle ourselves, including conflict resolution for anyone who wanted to share their issue. The challenge was that many teachers felt like the consequences for students exhibiting negative behavior were not punitive enough. It took some time for them to understand that a reflective process offered more opportunity for growth so that the student could be restored to the school community.

During this process, teacher relationships were strengthened because they got to share and really vent to each other about the challenges of moving toward restorative practices. The administration–teacher relationship was challenged because students were not punished according to the liking or philosophy of some of the teachers. In terms of suspensions and classroom misbehavior, the data really did speak to the struggles we went through as a school and how we achieved positive outcomes because we stuck with it. We had to reflect on our own personal philosophies and let go of many assumptions that had been holding us back. We had to give up our own ways of thinking and look at the data in meeting the needs of our students.

How relationships were challenged and yet grew.

We have students who have no adults they trust outside of school so we needed to become those adults. They needed to know that we would be advocates who cared for them and never gave up on them. Suspensions had never gotten to the root of the problem. We needed to connect them to resources for their mental health that would also support them as a whole person.

We have a 0% suspension rate and have embraced the restorative process because we see positive results. We still have students who misbehave in class but now teachers have built a community where they are able to have that one-on-one conversation and handle the issue themselves rather than sending the student out to admin. We still have teachers who struggle with some students and don't think they belong in a community; they resort to different strategies. But as a school we have overcome many challenges and now have a clear understanding of our discipline policy and how we address each child's needs.

New Thinking and Outcomes

As a school, our restorative justice practices have transformed our disciple matrix. Restoring the relationship that has been broken and giving students an opportunity to fix their error is a very powerful tool. We have seen wonderful outcomes as a result. Our small school with only 300–350 students has benefited because we created a community where they felt safe.

I have learned that every challenge in any organization needs to be diagnosed before it can be treated and fixed. We need an overall view (from the balcony) of the challenge and the people. I learned that trauma is about a loss of safety and so we built empathy in the staff by connecting them to how their own trauma has impacted them so that they could better understand the many traumas our students have experienced. I have learned to be patient and have those brave conversations. I have learned to take my administrator hat off, be vulnerable myself, and share my hidden truths and assumptions. I have learned to trust in the process and stay true to the relationships we have built as a team.

Case 3.9: Assistant Principal

The School Context

In our school, approximately 80% of our students are Latino/Hispanic and 20% are Black. We have a high number of students with special needs, many of whom are Black males. Additionally, we have a high number of ELL students, with an increase in newcomer students arriving from Mexico and Central America. Our school vision is to ensure that all students graduate with the skills they need to build lives of personal satisfaction, responsibility, and success. Our school mission is to become a dynamic learning community that fosters empathy, creativity, critical thinking, effective communication, and collaboration.

As an assistant principal, the scope of my job is never-ending. I am responsible for the overall safety of students and staff, athletics, facilities, special education, the PE department, the science department, school activities, campus aids, and campus security, all while supervising instruction and giving feedback to teachers. Key inspirational quotes that have helped shape my personal vision for the school are as follows:

> *"Education is the most powerful weapon, which you can use to change the world." —Nelson Mandela*

> *"You can't lead anyone if you can't lead yourself!"*
> *— Maxine Driscoll*

> *"If you're not making someone else's life better, then you are wasting your time. Your life will become better by making other people's lives better." — Will Smith*

> *"A leader takes people where they want to go. A great leader takes people where they don't necessarily want to go, but ought to be." — Rosalynn Carter*

The Adaptive Challenge

The adaptive challenge I tackled was how to shift from a punitive to a restorative justice way of looking at student behavior in the context of severe punishment being the norm? Restorative justice is very different from the detention/suspension system of the past. I chose this challenge (or it chose me!) because I am in charge of discipline. During our Western Association of Schools and Colleges (WASC) visit, the restorative justice policy was given some unfavorable reviews by staff in terms of its effectiveness. Some of the veteran teachers, and some who have more challenging students, felt that there were no consequences for continual behavior infractions. This made for a very conflict-oriented and tense environment.

What might the real challenge be here?

1. **We do not have the skills to meet the needs of students who challenge us academically and behaviorally.**
2. **Our systems have us trapped in a cycle of more severe punishment year after year instead of solving the underlining issues.**

The discipline committee is comprised of classroom teachers, counselors, the Dean, and myself. For this particular challenge, I offered to involve any classroom teacher who was interested in reviewing, revising, and revamping the current discipline plan. I also enlisted the district's Restorative Justice Team to train/retrain committee members on the core fundamentals of restorative justice so that they could all start with the same background information. Although we are still in the beginning stages, we have already seen a shift in some of the classroom teachers' comments about how the classroom environment has changed. Simply being aware of the empathy component gives them a better understanding of the importance of building relationships with students, as well as fellow staff members.

The first thing I asked of the teachers who joined the discipline committee was to review our current discipline policy. Then we all did the three-part restorative justice training (empathy, defusing disruptive behavior, and building community circles). Next, we met as a group to agree on levels of behavior intervention: Level 1 (teacher handles), Level 2 (counselor handles), and Level 3 (Dean/AP handles). Once these were arranged, I gave the work to the committee to revise, rewrite, or revamp the discipline policy. We planned to revisit and develop the policy based on feedback from the team.

I used the "get on the balcony" technique by asking teachers who disagreed with the restorative justice policy to work on the committee. I asked staff members who did not get along with co-workers to take a look at themselves (via the empathy training) and examine their part in that conflict. I also used the "hold steady" resource because after the training, the work was given back to the committee. If someone had an issue with the policy, then they were welcome to offer a solution rather than a complaint. Policy drafted with teacher input is more likely to be adhered to because of a sense of ownership, which could also get other faculty members to buy in.

This AP maintained and grew relationships by making others part of the process.

The key players in this adaptive challenge were the school counselors, my special education coordinator, the Dean of students, the teachers, and the restorative justice trainers. My value of equity was challenged by teachers who believed that only one type of punishment was appropriate for all repeat offenders. They seemed to think there should be some rubric for punishment, which is always punitive and does not actually influence a change of behavior. My values of trust and accountability were weakened because of a few teachers who refused to show empathy because of personal issues with other staff members. They could see neither their role in the conflict nor how the conflict could filter down to our students.

The work is never done! We must collect data and then return, diagnose, and work through the cycle again.

New Thinking and Outcomes

Since we continue to work through this challenge, our initial relationships have gotten stronger because we took the time to hear what the other team members were saying and feeling. We are making strides to ensure that, as a team, we develop a plan that benefits the students and gives them the skills needed to be successful in school. We also are working with the adults to understand their own triggers, which can escalate any situation (with another adult or a student). I learned that when people come together, they do not need to agree on everything but can still be productive and work towards a common goal. I also learned that everyone has something to contribute but needs to feel valued in order to participate.

Case 3.10:
Chief Operating Officer

The School Context

Our school is a public charter that serves a diverse student body with a primary demographic of African American students and large number of female students. Our mission is to prepare traditionally underserved students for success in the 21st century by providing a rigorous and relevant college-preparatory education that invests in talented human capital, provides early college experiences, and strives to adapt public education to the new millennium. The vision is to create empathetic, ethical, responsible, self-actualized, innovative citizens and provide an educational environment that empowers students, teachers, parents, and community through critical thinking, digital entrepreneurship, and collaboration, resulting in graduates who are college ready and clearly developed in both character and intellect. Our goal is to have the students create their own pathway to a four-year college program or vocational program while becoming outstanding citizens.

I am the chief operating officer, overseeing the financial health of the school. I am not limited to my job title because all our staff members have numerous responsibilities. These include assisting students with school-wide activities, maintaining the campus site, and managing office staff, payroll, human relations, purchasing, and personnel. I work closely with the principal and board members to manage campus responsibilities by preparing state and school district reports. Numerous inspirational quotes help define my personal vision for this work:

> "Let Your Life Speak"
> — a Quaker saying that has informed my life

> "Our deepest fear is not that we are inadequate. Our deepest fear is that we are powerful beyond measure. It is our light, not our darkness, that most frightens us. Your playing small does not serve the world." — Timo Cruz

> "Help others achieve their dreams and you will achieve yours." — Les Brown

The Adaptive Challenge

The school enrollment projected for the 2017–2018 school year was 205 students. The enrollment at the start of the school year was 167 students, which increased to 176, but remained well below the projected 205. I choose this adaptive challenge, because I felt the impact would force us to make major cuts to our budget for the school year. We had to reflect on the issue of low enrollment and then increase enrollment for the upcoming school year.

The participants in this adaptive challenge were our school administration team, both classified and certificated staff, which consisted of the principal, assistant principal, college counselors, Dean of students, teachers, registrar, office

Is this an adaptive challenge? Increasing enrollment can be done by recruitment, so the skills necessary to do this should already be in place. This issue needs to be drilled down further to find the real adaptive challenge. It could be as broad as not having the skills necessary to review data about all aspects of our school in order to improve it.

clerk, and myself. I felt it was very important to include the whole staff, because this adaptive challenge required a lot of brainstorming, feedback, and action planning. We also involved the student body, which allowed the students to become creative and promote their school in a positive light. We were able to utilize the students' creativity along with the staff ideas to increase our school enrollment and improve our recruiting plans for the next school year.

This is an innovation — or hack.

Using data from previous school years, we were able to critically analyze practices that our previous administrative team had used to recruit students. The team were able to track the data based on student demographics, which included race/ethnicity, grade level, gender, attendance, and geography. The focus changed from planning to implementing a new way to recruit as a team. The team was able to narrow down the areas to focus on utilizing professional development time to work on the new recruiting action plan. Everyone was assigned a role, which was included in the action plan. Staff involvement allowed us to make everyone feel comfortable in providing feedback to create change. The action plan created an open dialog, reflection, and collaboration among our staff. The adaptive challenge allowed us to continue utilizing the tools we learned through this process.

Taking on this adaptive challenge allowed us to strengthen our commitment to students and parents to keep the school open and functioning, with a renewed partnership between the staff and the administration team. We challenged the notion that recruiting is a job only for certain staff members. It grew into a school-wide challenge to bring new students and parents to our campus. It gave everyone on staff the ability to unify around a common goal, thereby strengthening our team unity and community rather than our individualism.

Some of the relationships were challenging in the beginning, but were strengthened through understanding how this benefitted the whole school and through the collaborative work on the adaptive challenge. This ultimately resulted in a system of greater accountability and a clearer communication path between administrators and teachers, and between certificated and classified staff. Overall, working through this challenge allowed us, as a team, to strengthen our relationships. Since there were many positive outcomes, we must assume that lots of great relationship building, collaboration, and commitment happened by design.

Since there were many positive outcomes, we must assume that lots of great relationship building, collaboration, and commitment happened by design.

New Thinking and Outcomes

Working through this adaptive challenge helped to release the negative attitudes that people originally brought to the table. Everybody realized that it is their job to recruit parents and students. We also shed our severe individualism on campus and became more of a cohesive team where we began to value the success of our fellow team members as we valued our own success, seeing the two as interdependent. We have been able, through our resolution of the adaptive challenge, to implement new recruitment practices. The staff now have a cohesive approach to recruiting and are willing to focus on what needs to be done.

Showing the staff a more positive outlook helped me to strengthen these relationships. I now witness more positive attitudes from our staff and less of the "me first" attitude. This ultimately brought about a cultural change, from an individualistic approach to a collective one for goal setting and success. This shift has greatly strengthened our team and has allowed us all to better unify around the mission/vision of our school. I will take what I have learned from working through this adaptive challenge and apply the tools to whatever new adaptive challenges we face as a school, which can only change our collective environment for the better.

Case 3.11:
Guidance Counselor

The School Context

Our mission and vision is focused on developing creative and critical thinkers who are contributing members of society using interdisciplinary, rigorous curriculum with arts integration. Since we became a magnet school four years ago, our diverse student population continues to grow every year. We currently have four buses transporting students from different areas of our county. This increase in diversity has positively impacted our school, enriching our culture, creativity, talent, and language. As a performing arts magnet school, we are committed to addressing and working on the social justice issues affecting our school and the surrounding community. We have partners, such as United Students, who address and find ways to tackle the social justice issues affecting our students and their families.

As a guidance counselor, I am constantly seeking ways to promote cultural awareness among students and staff. As a member of the community, I am aware of the social justice issues affecting the school community and beyond. This awareness allows me to tackle issues when they arise. As a stakeholder, it is my job to ensure that my work with the students and staff is aligned with our school's mission and vision. One of the more inspirational quotes that affects my personal vision of the work is this:

> *"Success is no accident. It is hard work, perseverance, learning, studying, sacrifice and most of all, love of what you are doing or learning to do."* — Pelé

The Adaptive Challenge

The adaptive challenge I chose to undertake deals with mathematics. Approximately 65% of our 9th graders were failing Algebra 1 by the week 10 report card in the fall. By the final report card in December, 40% had failed. This is unacceptable, and despite a supportive teacher and tutoring offered every day, the 9th graders still failed. The reason I chose this challenge was because I felt that if we did not intervene, these 9th graders would continue to fail and create a culture of failure.

In order to tackle this problem, we made sure to involve the math teacher, the students who failed in the fall, the assistant principal, parents, tutors, and senior mentors. We met with parents and students, adapted mastery grading, and modified the work for the students who were failing. We put students on mandatory tutoring contracts and a math contract. The math contract stated that as long as they did all the lab work on the Delta Math program and passed each Delta Math test, they would be able to pass the Algebra 1 class with a D or C; if they wanted a higher grade, they would need to pass the chapter tests as well.

How do we ensure that students can successfully complete Algebra? Since large failure rates are common at many high schools and Algebra is the gatekeeper to college, this is not only an academic challenge but an equity challenge.

Students were monitored weekly. Those progressing did not have to meet with the teacher and counselor. However, those who continued to fail had meetings twice a week. The assistant principal was a key player since she supported the idea of having student contracts, adapting mastery grading, and modifying the work. The teacher noticed that many of the students who were failing lacked basic math knowledge, which is why they had difficulty understanding the concepts in Algebra 1. When the students began working on the modified version of Delta Math, their confidence and progress in math increased. Now the number of students failing at the 10 week report card has decreased significantly.

The hack has some success — time to collect data and begin again!

New Thinking and Outcomes

What I learned from this challenge was that as educators, administrators, and support staff, we have to work together to find a solution, especially when we have such a large number of students failing a class. Tackling the problem immediately is key. The lesson for all of us working on this challenge is to ensure that we work on a solution as soon as we have preliminary grades, not wait until final grades.

Case 3.12:
Principal and ILT Team

The School Context

The mission of our school is to provide all students with opportunities missed earlier in their education to master grade-level proficiency and to ensure that every student reaches 21st century skills through academic performance and social opportunities. We give students an opportunity to enhance their critical thinking, collaborative, communication, and creative skills. With a multifaceted system of support and intervention, we pledge to work with the students and their families to realize these outcomes. We believe students will develop the 21st century skills needed to be a successful, socially responsible, respectful, self-disciplined human being with positive behaviors and attitudes.

During orientation week in the fall, all students participate in Project Silver Lining. This is a holistic, multidisciplinary project incorporating yoga, mindfulness training, film, and visual arts. The program is structured to work with at-promise youth and introduce them to the arts as an effective means to access their own voices, transform their attitudes, and envision their futures. Concepts of trust and respect, personal development, and social responsibility are at the core of this program, which is designed to engage students in exploring the meaning of personal and collective action in their lives and in their community.

In our Identity Project, we have students define their identity through their race/ethnicity and their inherited or socially constructed identities. This project incorporates reading material and film that include themes of race and culture. Students culminate their learning through an art or film piece.

Our ILT team was comprised of three educators: 1) social studies teacher/community based learning facilitator; 2) principal/speech teacher/Spanish teacher; and 3) math/science/case based learning facilitator. We drew inspiration from quotations such as these:

"Pressure makes diamonds." — Unknown

"Teaching is a work of heart." — Unknown

*"Learn something new... then teach someone."
— Unknown*

*"A boy comes to me with a spark of interest. I feed the spark and it becomes a flame. I feed the flame and it becomes a fire. I feed the fire and it becomes a roaring blaze."
— Constantine D'Amato*

The Adaptive Challenge

A challenge we have worked through at our school has been establishing a school culture that facilitates a safe learning environment where students feel welcomed and taken care of. We have created a culture of self-care and self-compassion through mindfulness practices embedded into our bell schedule. Since we serve at-promise youth, the majority of whom qualify for free or reduced lunch, these students enter the school dealing with a myriad of socioeconomic and socio-emotional issues. Mindfulness practices are one way that we can help students deal with their emotions and frustrations. Our staff chose to address this challenge because we realized that before any form of academic learning can take place, we must first ensure the emotional well-being of our students. This begins by providing them with a safe learning environment that is welcoming and understanding of (their problems). Mindfulness practices are a healthy avenue for students to relieve some of the stress they are dealing with.

> **How can we create conditions for learning for the most disenfranchised and marginalized students whose life challenges far outweigh the school's ability to ensure their comfort, safety, and support? The challenge might include creating spaces for learning in new ways to meet the needs of marginalized students who have suffered at school.**

Before implementing mindfulness practices, all staff members received extensive professional development. As part of the training, staff received

DVDs, electronic resources, and thumb drives containing resources on brain-based research as well as movements to practice at school and at home to develop healthy minds and bodies. The staff went right to work implementing these practices during the school day, 15 minutes before our lunch period.

We quickly realized that one day of PD training was not enough since students were resisting the practices. To deal with the lack of staff training and student buy in, we allocated additional days of training for instructors, students, and staff members to work directly with mindfulness instructors. These workshops were beneficial in persuading some of the resistant students, as they demonstrated that all school stakeholders were truly open to learning something new, something different that places us outside of our comfort zone.

In order to get to this place, all staff members engaged in discussions regarding the struggles we were facing in the classroom. Some staff members were on the verge of giving up and siding with the reluctant students. It was very important that all staff members and students buy into the practice in order for mindfulness to become embedded in our school culture. Any breaks in the chain were sure to throw off the entire program, so reflection on the practices from both students and staff was valued and encouraged. Having open conversations about the mindfulness integration process, listening to student perceptions of its usefulness, and hearing other thoughts or concerns were important, especially if the goal was to provide students with the confidence needed to transfer over to the academic part of schooling.

Our lead staff members were important players as we navigated our way through this adaptive challenge. Additionally, certified mindfulness trainers were critical in the sustainability of our program. All staff members agree that mindfulness is an active part of our curriculum, our school culture, and is here to stay. Prospective students are informed of our practices; if they are unwilling to participate, they are encouraged to find a different school. For the most part, we have met little to no resistance from new students, as all current students are engaged in mindfulness in one form or another.

Part of what made this challenge difficult to implement in the beginning was that students were not given a choice as to whether or not mindfulness was something that they wanted to embark upon. Our top-down approach was accepted and adopted by staff members because many had already practiced breathing, stretching, and reflective practices at some point in their lives and had achieved positive results.

What interesting data could be collected during this process?

Initially, students did not respond well to being forced to do mindful practices. The resistance was especially visible in some classrooms and those teachers considered dropping mindfulness or advocated that participation be voluntary. But voluntary participation would undermine the program, so this was simply not an option.

In order to assist teachers having a difficult time, we took two important steps. First, we held a general assembly to let everyone know that mindfulness was not optional and that all students were expected to participate. Disruptions during mindfulness time would not be tolerated. Second, students were given options. Practices held in specific rooms would vary by staff member, with some instructors focusing on energizing, calming, or walking practices. Thus, students could choose where and how to practice mindfulness. Students who were still unwilling to participate and accept this part of our school culture were asked to look into an alternate school.

New Thinking and Outcomes

Mindfulness has strengthened our school's mission of engaging learners through a student-centered approach. While students still make comments about their hippie teachers and their breathing exercises, they are aware of the brain-based research that encourages mental breaks and reducing stress and anxiety. An increased number of students are now open to discussing their thoughts and feelings during our weekly community circles.

Relationships between teachers and students have also been strengthened through mindfulness since students and teachers are both learners and practitioners of self-care. Teachers have expressed that when they are feeling stressed and unaware of their changing behavior, students are quick to call them out on their mood and suggest they take some time to be "mindful." Additionally, when students are not actively participating in mindfulness, it is usually a clue for teachers to make sure they are feeling okay. Sure enough, upon approaching non-participants, teachers become aware of a student having a bad day or not feeling well. Overall, mindfulness and community circles have increased communication between students and staff that has ultimately strengthened relationships and created a climate of caring.

Case 3.13: Principal

The School Context

Our school students, grades 9 through 12, are primarily located in a large urban school district. Our demographics shifted when we moved from one city to another. Due to the origin of the school in a city with a large African American community and presence, our school was able to build a name for itself within that community. That reputation traveled with our school in the move to the second city where the school still has a high enrollment of African American students. This move has also enabled us to establish ourselves in the Latino community so our school has been able to see that student demographic increase.

The school continues to meet the needs of the community through various clubs that students can participate in during lunch and after school. Academic drive is encouraged in all of them, including Homework, Writing Lab, and Botany. Other clubs such as Basketball, Soccer, Glee, Art, Anime, Gay Straight Alliance, and Poetry give the students many educational outlets.

We utilize the student success team process to further support the school's tiered intervention team in conjunction with the Positive Behavioral Interventions and Supports (PBIS) school-wide system to further support students who have been targeted as highest need (tier III) for behavior/academic intervention and support. The SST team process consists of a unified team of each targeted student, their teachers, guardians, counselors, and various other wrap-around service members deemed necessary for their adequate support. The SST team develops and applies targeted interventions in both academics and behaviors with the ultimate goal of supporting high-need students in their efforts to meet their behavior and academic goals. The team monitors and tracks all interventions and adjusts them appropriately until the student is adequately supported.

Our school's vision is to create empathetic, ethical, responsible, self-actualized, innovative citizens and provide an educational environment that empowers students, teachers, parents, and community through critical thinking, digital entrepreneurship, and collaboration, resulting in graduates who are college ready and clearly developed in both character and intellect. This is an ongoing process of consistently trying every intervention to meet the needs of the individual student in order to help them succeed. We must try every intervention possible or we have failed as a school.

My job consists of being an instructional leader, creating a positive school culture for the students, organizational leadership, financial and business leadership (budget), hiring personnel, and community outreach. My aim is to keep a healthy balance between all these things, but many times the intricacies of each role make the balance difficult. My personal vision for my work focuses on what I hope will be the safest, most authentic, critically engaging school experience for students. Ultimately, I want students to feel empowered, to have a voice, and to change the status quo of what is expected of them. If we can empower students to question everything and stand firmly then we help them become contributing adults in society. Numerous quotes have helped define me, including the following:

"Education is the passport to the future, for tomorrow belongs to those who prepare for it today." — Malcolm X

"The function of education is to teach one to think intensively and to think critically. Intelligence plus character — that is the goal of true education."
— Martin Luther King, Jr.

"No matter who you are, no matter what you did, no matter where you've come from, you can always change; become a better version of yourself." — Madonna

The Adaptive Challenge

The adaptive challenge I hacked and worked through focused on student voice. For students to feel empowered, they must first feel that they have a voice. A constantly punitive school environment will not produce a wealth of respect and love. Over the last couple of years, we needed to transform from a punitive campus to a positive behavior intervention campus. We needed to change from a "don't do that" campus to more of a relationship-building campus.

This is a very interesting adaptive challenge and way of looking at the challenge.

It was evident in the 2013–2014 school year when we lost 10 staff members that instability ruled and our students were unhappy. We needed a great shift in the overall culture of the school. So we asked ourselves this question: How do we change and intervene and help students in a positive way that would better empower them to have a voice, make critical decisions, and be able to analyze why their actions occurred? I think many schools face this challenge with staff — from teachers to office staff to administration. The principal, the Dean, the teachers, and I (assistant principal) were all involved. It has only been in the last couple of years that we've had enough stability in personnel to fully commit ourselves to investing in PBIS.

We formed a PBIS team this year with our lead teacher, our special education coordinator, and me. However, the teachers themselves would be leading the charge in the classroom with restorative justice circles, model warrior incentives, and PBIS events. These interventions needed to be played out through the dialogue that teachers have on a daily basis with students. They also needed to run deep through the front offices, the counseling office, and everyone else coming into contact with the students.

Our lead teachers and members of our instructional leadership team met with the teachers and we revamped our PLC groups. We used our summer PD as a chance to instill vital components of PBIS. Teachers needed to analyze how they were building a PBIS culture in their classrooms. Walkthroughs and a chance to have check-in meetings to see what was being implemented helped in the overall school analysis. We also told our college professors about our culture so they could help with the students too.

Key players were added as we progressed, including the administration, the Leadership Instructional Team, teachers, office staff, and parents. Students were to be at the center, so they were the main reason for the adaptive challenge. However, the biggest challenge would be the adults implementing the initiative. The challenge was getting every staff member on the same page. We asked ourselves and each other "Why do you teach?" Are you here to implement every intervention possible? Are you here to send a student out of class at the drop of a hat? Are you here with a punitive mindset or a restorative mindset? Reflecting on certain discipline situations allowed the staff to review the outcomes and also look at other possible ways of handling things. The more scenarios we played out in professional development, the more growth occurred in the staff. Additionally, collaborating with certain students in mind allowed the teachers to gain a better understanding of what was happening in their classroom verses their peers' classrooms. Peer observations allowed for growth also. Constantly asking "Why do I teach?" brought out the true mindset of teachers, what they value about their jobs, and what they value in their students.

Using an interesting hack, "Why do you teach?"

New Thinking and Outcomes

Relationships between the administration and the lead teachers were strengthened and the most important relationship of all —between students and their teachers — was also strengthened. Through peer collaboration, teachers were able to shift their educational philosophy on discipline. Perhaps it has been resolved completely because PBIS can always be implemented further. It is never "over" as new people come into our school and learn what we are trying to do for our students. The most important point, however, is that the shift has happened. PBIS is in every classroom to different degrees. There is more of a restorative purpose behind discipline. Because of that, we can say that the implementation has been a success.

When people collaborate, relationships are strengthened.

I have learned that if you want change, you must work for it. Nothing happens overnight. Being on the same page as your staff is of utmost importance. If that happens, then change can happen.

Case 3.14:
Instructional Coach

The School Context

At our school, we believe in using restorative practices to build community with our students to help them be successful. We have striven to create a college- and career-ready culture through the implementation of a dedicated advisory program, building literacy skills through close reading, and using mastery learning and EDI to support rigorous instruction. Our student demographic is predominantly Hispanic, with a 5% African American population, and it operates on a shared campus with three other schools. Our school is also a Pilot School where we have autonomy over certain areas, such as staffing, curriculum, and budget.

As the Instructional Coach, my primary responsibility is to facilitate the implementation of mastery learning at our school. One of the main areas I support is providing professional development for teachers in Mastery Learning and providing instructional support as they develop and implement their lessons. Additionally, I also support the data analysis and intervention programs at my school to ensure that students who are struggling are identified and we can provide support. Lastly, I also work with the Advisory Leads to develop and implement the curriculum for our Advisory Program.

My personal vision is shaped greatly by the philosophy of Response to Intervention (RTI), which states that it is our duty as educators to "ensure all students can learn and learn at high levels." I believe in preparing our students for the future by ensuring they have a solid academic foundation, while also showing them the possibilities of the future. Lastly, I believe "students first, content second." I believe it is important to see my students for who they are as people so that I can best help them learn.

The Adaptive Challenge

I chose the adaptive challenge of adopting mastery learning and grading practices as the area I hacked and worked through. Our students were consistently failing classes due to not submitting assignments. When teachers were asked why the students were struggling, their response was that they "knew the students knew the material, but were not turning in their work." For their part, students were unable to articulate why they were struggling in their classes.

Diagnosing the adaptive challenge takes time. If something is mandated to occur the adaptive challenge might be this: How can we fully train and assist all teachers and staff with the implementation of an initiative with our current values, culture, and knowledge so that all are successful when we have never had this experience and do not know how to do it?

Who and What Did I Bring to the Challenge?

Besides myself, my principal, assistant principal, Leadership Team, and teachers from multiple disciplines were involved in the initiative. The person who was added was a mastery learning and grading facilitator who helped facilitate the professional development series for our teachers.

The tools I used to work on my challenge were the book *Immunity to Change* (Kegan & Lahey, 2009) as a way of thinking about why teachers were resistant to the change. I also used the ideas presented in *Leadership on the Line* (Heifetz & Linsky, 2017) as I planned professional development and thought about ways to address the issues teachers were facing. I also used *The Choreography of Presenting* (Zoller & Landry, 2010) to develop engaging professional development for the teachers.

How Did We Create and Innovate?

First, I spoke with my principal and our Leadership Team about the successes we had with our first two groups of teachers who implemented mastery learning. I also led a professional development workshop during the summer where teachers read an article about a student from Jefferson High School who struggled during his first year in college. I showed our students' college acceptance rates and compared them to our students' college continuation rates to show how even our high-performing students were struggling in post-secondary.

Next, I worked with the district's Mastery Learning and Grading Department and convinced them to hold a training series on our school site. I also had to convince my principal and our School Site Council to fund time for our teachers to attend the trainings on Saturdays. Once the training was over, the real work began. The teachers understood the philosophy of mastery learning and grading, but were struggling with the technical aspects of adopting the new grading model. Therefore, I had to adjust our PD plan to ensure that students understood the technical aspects of the work.

We are now in our first year of school-wide implementation of mastery learning and grading, having 17 of our 21 teachers certified as Mastery Learning Teachers. Teachers were then able to identify learning targets for their content areas and align their digital gradebook to their learning targets. Currently, all our teachers have implemented some form of mastery learning and grading, however, there is still a lot of work to be done in aligning our assessments and curriculum.

New Thinking and Outcomes

One of the values that we strengthened was "trust." Teachers trusted our vision and that our Leadership Team had the knowledge and skills to implement a new instructional model of grading. Another value that grew was collaboration because our teachers were able to discuss and meet with each other to develop common grading practices. Some relationships were challenged between the "old school" teachers and those who believe in social justice and equity. Relationships grew between our grade level teams and the department teams as they engaged in data discussions and unit planning.

Data collection is essential for evidence-based change.

The main thing we lost was the excuse to say that students "know" or "don't know" something without evidence. Our new challenge is that we now have many new teachers at our school, meaning we have to reinvest time in shifting philosophies about grading. Our professional development schedule will be readjusted and our five-year plan will now become a six-year plan.

I learned a lot from this process. First, shifting mindsets is difficult; people have core values they believe in and will resort back to these. The process also reaffirmed my belief that you "have to move the elephant before you can move the rider." I also learned how important it is to "give the work back" to the people who need to implement it. My teachers were more invested and empowered when we used the ideas from the books we read together. Lastly, I learned that plans will change and change takes time. And that's okay too.

Case 3.15:
Special Education Teacher

The School Context

Our school is located in a low socioeconomic area in the heart of gang community — three gangs in particular. Most of our students are of Hispanic heritage and the majority live on or below the poverty line. We have developed Restorative Practices on campus as our social justice system. Our vision and mission for the school is to provide an arts education to all students, making sure each one graduates with the skills of being a student, a citizen, and an artist. We are a college-ready school that emphasizes high expectations for all students. Through standards-based grading, Councils, and Arts Pathways, we expect each student to develop goals and aspirations to be ready for college and to go to college.

I am a Resource Specialist Program (RSP) teacher at the school working with one other RSP teacher. We co-teach in English and Math and develop plans to ensure that each of our students with special needs, as well as other students who are struggling, are provided with the support and accommodations needed to succeed in the classroom. I am also the lead teacher of the 11th grade College Prep Seminar courses so I develop curriculum and help new teachers implement the curriculum. I am also part of the Restorative Practices (RP) committee, which tries to guide teachers to better understanding how restorative justice works. We present professional development on how to effectively implement restorative practices. Finally, I was part of the Design Team; part of the original eight who founded the school and brought it to where it is now. My personal vision for the work is highly connected to the following quotes:

> *"We make a living by what we get, but we make a life by what we give." — Winston Churchill*

> *"In the field of education, we give to our students. We make a life out of what we give and how we give it. This is my life. I was born to help, to think about others, and*

to make sure that others grow and become the best person they can possibly be." — Unknown

"To plant a garden is to believe in tomorrow."
— Audrey Hepburn

"Be thou the rainbow to the storms of life. The evening beam that smiles the clouds away, And tints tomorrow with prophetic ray." — Lord Byron

In education, we are planting a garden. When we opened our school, we planted a garden in the community; a garden in a city that needed to see something new grow. Our design, our implementation, and our first years needed a great deal of watering and care. We needed to make sure that our plants were sprouting. Each year we get new seedlings (freshmen) who need to know that at our school, we will not give up. We expect the seedlings not only to grow, but to grow strong and pass on their knowledge and hope to those who come to the school after them. As teachers, we water and feed this garden so that everyone at the school flourishes.

I am the rainbow in the storm of life. Or at least I try to be. Because of where I teach, in a community of students who sometimes feel trapped and pushed down every day by their home life, or their poverty level, or whatever barriers they have tried to get past, I have to show them that there is hope. I try to show them that I care about them, even when they get in trouble. I make sure they know that I am not going to give up on them. Teaching students with learning disabilities is particularly challenging, because I have to help them emotionally as well as academically. I have to guide them to know that they have intelligences in them. That they need to find out what works for them, and to use their own strategies to learn. I want every student to succeed and, even though motivating them is very draining and difficult at times, I feel that they eventually begin to find that hope and motivation within themselves.

The Adaptive Challenge

This past school year, we decided to implement standards-based grading throughout the school. We immediately realized how effective it is in challenging students to show that they are learning the material.

The technical challenge is implementing a grading system. The adaptive challenges may include how to create a school culture where students value their work and respond in positive ways to a new grading system.

Points were no longer used to grade; instead, students were graded on mastery of a standard. The philosophy behind standards-based grading was obvious, but the reactions and changes that it brought to the student mindset were challenging for everyone involved. I chose this challenge because I immediately saw how a large change in a school could affect everyone involved. The entire school was involved — students, parents, teachers, staff, families, and administration. I saw the positive side of implementing standards-based grading because it was shown to be highly effective in making sure students were actually learning the material. However, for the students, especially the seniors, this change had a huge impact on their future because it effected their grades in ways they were not used to.

When standards-based grading was implemented at the beginning of the year, teachers were not fully ready for the implementation. They knew what they had to do, but weren't entirely clear on how to do it. Different classes had different methods. One class had percentages, while another had 1's, 2's, and 3's for grades. After changing from a 1–4 grading scale, the students were completely confused and stressed. They did not know how to read their grades on the Schoology learning management system (LMS).

When teachers feel they lack knowledge or competence, it can create resistance and have other negative collateral outcomes. The adaptive challenge was not in implementing the program, but rather in creating a culture of continuous learning.

As a special education teacher who sees things from the outside, I was unable to figure out how to explain it to the students. Parents complained about all the fails their child was getting when they used to be an A or B student. Parents started pulling their children out of the school and our enrollment dropped. Seniors were leaving because they were failing. The office staff had to deal with phone calls from complaining parents. The administration was trying to keep the teachers on board with the movement to standards-based grading. They were trying to explain it to the parents as best they could, but got trapped in the fact that we hadn't really developed a clear picture to begin with. Teachers were trying to make it clear to students, but were also struggling. One group of teachers was trying the new system, while another group decided to stick to their original grading system.

In order to combat the discrepancies in what we wanted standards-based grading to look like, and how to implement it, a standards-based grading committee was established. Faculty voted and those who wanted to use standards-based grading would join the committee and figure it out together; those who did not would use their own grading system for the year. Anyone could be on the committee, if they were willing to put in the extra time to develop a plan on how to show the students their growth without having them feel discouraged about their grade. Parents were also informed of the change and invited to conference with teachers so the teacher could explain the grading process. The committee created a diagram for parents to show them how the grades would look on Schoology.

One of the values that was challenged was our integrity as a school. We were losing students because we looked unorganized. Teachers had to defend themselves to parents and students. We also lost trust with the students, especially our seniors. Once one student left the school, then others followed because they were scared of not graduating. Trust was lost between parents, students, and faculty, but at the same time, I think trust was gained between teachers. We all felt that we had to keep our heads above water as a team or sink together. We had to defend each other and assure the students that we were doing a good thing. By second semester, the committee had formed a plan that was spelled out to the students.

The hardest relationships to keep were with the parents and the seniors. They challenged us regularly, pointing out the flaws in rolling out this grading system when Schoology was brand new. The seniors had gone through a flawed grading system that allowed them to get passing grades even though they really didn't know the content of the class. The relationships between the administration and teachers were also strained. Teachers had to fight off complaining students and felt the brunt of the problem was on them. Administration had to fight off parents and felt the brunt of the problem was on them. Everyone was on edge and bitter towards one another.

Relationships were strengthened, however, between new teachers and those who had been at the school a while. Our many new incoming teachers were very knowledgeable about standards-based grading. They saw firsthand how the old grading system did not show that students learned anything and were very frustrated in the classroom because students had such low skills. This was obvious in the math classes, where juniors in Algebra 2 did not have basic Algebra 1 skills. The new teachers wanted the change and jumped on board with enthusiasm to make them. This strengthened the relationship between administration and teachers because it brought everyone together for a greater purpose. Many of our teachers are very competitive and did not want to see our ship sink.

We lost some good students. Seniors who were going to college. Juniors who were college bound and had a great deal of promise. Performers in dance, theater, music, and art, who were exceptional. Being an art school, this was a significant blow to our art teachers. We lost our reputation in the community. When students started leaving, other students followed. We were no longer perceived as an art school, but rather as an unorganized institution that did not seem to care about the students' futures. We had to persevere because we knew that this change was for the best, creating a stronger grading system that would truly foster student learning.

New Thinking and Outcomes

This change happened quickly, which, in a way, is good. We still have some kinks to work out, but in the end I believe we have prevailed. Most students came to realize that they need to show they are learning in order to pass a course. Teachers have offered tutoring throughout the week and during lunch to make sure that students are given plenty of opportunities to resubmit their work. Students are using terminology associated with standards-based grading and are realizing that they have plenty of opportunity to show mastery of the skill. They realize that just because they fail a test in the first half of the semester does not mean they are doomed for the rest of the semester. It is not about averages, it is about growth. We have all settled down as a school. No one seems as stressed out anymore and we, as teachers, are able to see the growth that is taking place. The students are held accountable for their learning and are showing us that they are learning the material. They are not able to work the system anymore. We are preparing them for college and the real world where hard work is needed to succeed. Students are no longer leaving the school because of the grading system. I believe our reputation might end up getting stronger since we will no longer be looked at as the easy art school. We will be looked at as the Art Magnet in the valley that pushes their students to become college ready.

We learned a great deal through this process. We learned to trust our instincts and continue to strive for our desired outcomes despite the inevitable bumps along the way. We learned that if we want to implement something, we need to have a plan first. We need to have communications that are easy for parents, students, teachers, and office staff to understand. We need to have a school-wide awareness campaign before diving into a tremendous change, so that everyone is aware and ready. Changing the mindset *before* changing the system is essential when proposing a solution. We should have had a parent meeting, inviting parents to give us their perspectives and participate in our roll out.

We also learned that the integrity and reputation of the school is more important than each individual's motives. We decided as a faculty to adapt our school to a better, more effective learning environment for our students, and we came together during a downturn to prove that what we were doing was worth it. With every change comes pushback. There are bumps in the road and obstacles that, at the time, seem insurmountable. We learned to never give up on ourselves as a school. We believe what our school is essential to the community, and we want to give everything we can to help our students succeed. This will not be the last change we make in this school, but we now know how to make the next change much smoother.

> Changing the grading system is a technical fix, which does not reflect on whether the change is good or bad. What is important is to ensure that the grading system, when implemented, addresses the challenge. As you reflect on this narrative, identify what *you* think the adaptive challenge is that will be addressed by a standards-based grading system.

Case 3.16: Assistant Principal

The School Context

My school is nestled in an urban community in southern California. The school is co-located on a campus with two other district schools and two independent charter schools. The high school is a community school serving all families in the surrounding area who select to attend our school via zone of choice.

My role began as the EL/Title I coordinator and now I serve as assistant principal. Due to our co-location with the charter schools, our high school has always had a higher enrollment of English Learners (EL) students and Special Education (SPED) students, as the charter schools do not always accept them. My vision has always been to provide students in this community with the best education possible to prepare them for entering either college or the work force ready to be successful. As an individual who grew up in this community, I take my role very seriously.

The Adaptive Challenges

One of our challenges over the last few years is getting the teaching staff to understand the complexity of teaching to our subgroups. The majority of our students are Latino with consistently 26% EL, 22% SPED, and roughly 50% Reclassified Fluent English Proficient (RFEP). Over the years, data have shown that our subgroups are not meeting their instructional progress targets and there is a high fail rate for core classes; even the RFEP students are performing poorly on standardized tests.

> **Step #4** — The initial phase of recognizing an adaptive challenge is anchored in beliefs. In this case, faculty believed that the way they teach was sufficient for the students they served.

During the summer of 2016, I ran the summer school credit recovery program and I was lucky enough to participate in "mastery teaching and grading" training in preparation. I was immediately in contact with my principal about how we could bring the training to our staff in order to tackle the high fail rate problem. If our school needed to enroll 60 students in Biology during the summer because they failed the course and we had only 85 students enrolled in the course during the year, this was urgent. As a small school, we could not afford to continue with such a high fail rate and we had to address many questions. Why were students failing? What supports were teachers providing for students in danger of failing? What interventions did we need to provide for our students?

As we began the 2016–2017 school year, we presented our staff with the data. The coordinator and I led our teachers in activities that allowed them to discover who our students are, how they had been performing, how many courses they were failing, and how that impacted our master schedule. We kept it low key, one piece at a time, one discussion at a time. By the end of the two days, teachers started to ask for ideas on

> **Step #5** — A safe learning environment where the adults could discover what they needed.

Case Narratives

how to improve what we had identified as a pressing concern. We were ready to respond with a plan of action: Training all teachers on mastery teaching and grading. Saturday training was available and teachers were paid overtime to attend. All we asked was for them to commit to the training, implement some strategies, and observe each other through learning walks. All staff participated and we used tools provided to us through the Innovative School Leadership Institute (ISLI) to structure our learning walks, document the data, record our findings, and hold professional discussions on our work. Everyone was on board.

Our biggest challenge was the district mandated grade book portal. It did not lend itself to setting up grading systems any different from the 0–100 point traditional grading scale. At first, teachers were willing to set up their own grade book separate from the district required one. But this meant two separate grade books, and double the work during grading windows. Throughout the year, two teachers took the lead in experimenting with the grade book portal and then sharing how they are managing to keep up with mastery grading in their classes.

An attempted hack.

By June of 2017, the rest of the teachers had tried their best but many had given up and gone back to their old ways of traditional grading. As part of the closing of the 2016–2017 school year, we decided to do more PD on mastery grading and work together to identify how we could refocus and tighten tasks a little better to increase our success. We looked at the data and identified three school-wide strategies to implement: 1) eliminate the 0–100 grading scale, 2) get rid of the zero, and 3) grade on a standards-based proficiency rubric that we would create together. With that, we went off for summer vacation. Then they lowered the boom on us, literally!

The failure of the hack illustrated that the problem was not actually with grade reporting.

Two weeks prior to the start of the next school year, we were notified that we would be merging with the other pilot high school on the campus. Needless to say, our PD schedule went out the window as our focus shifted completely. That year, all of our time and energy went into building trust and bringing two completely separate staffs together. At first, we thought it was impossible, but thanks to all the resources we had gathered through ISLI, we made great progress. We were used to competing with the other school and they were used to functioning under a very different mission and vision. They were reluctant to work with our students, only wanting their students in their classes. We are still working at it, but I have to say that I'm really proud of the fact that right now, we are one school, working together in amazingly collaborative ways.

They used data to come up with a few solutions (grading), which did not work. This failure (outside their influence) then thrust them into a new ecotone — increased diversity of thought, values, and beliefs. They now have tools for creating community and they continue to be in the midst of their ecotone. They are presently focusing on building an adult community where trust can be established.

Case 3.17: Assistant Principal

The School Context

Our school is located in an impoverished community of a large urban school district. Our mission is to ensure that our students are college ready and successfully matriculate through college in 4–5 years. As world changers, our students will be able to come back to their communities and make sustainable positive changes. Our students have been underserved in their local district elementary and middle schools and usually come to us 4–6 grade levels behind. As a school, we are committed to increasing students' hope, pathways knowledge, and literacy levels by graduation.

As a founding teacher, I have seen this school grow and develop over it first eight years. Now as an assistant principal, I am eager to push our academic programs and develop our teacher leaders. As the AP of instruction, testing, and curriculum, my main job is supporting and coaching teachers. Although I work directly with teachers, I am also closely connected to student achievement. My work and vision are informed by the following question: "Are the children well?" Keeping our students first and over serving those previously underserved has always been my personal mantra for teaching. When I first came to teaching, I was eager to serve African American students and excited when hired to teach in this community. Although our demographics have changed, I have learned that my passion is not just for African American students but also "at-hope" students. This keeps me inspired as I serve in my community. Every day I hope to be able to say that our children are well.

The Adaptive Challenge

The following symptoms really outline our adaptive challenge: In the first three months of school we lost four 9th grade teachers, two ELA teachers, one PE teacher, and our Human Geography teacher. As well, our 9th grade Spanish teacher was out on maternity leave. In any given day, a student could have 100% substitute teachers. This left a void and inconsistency in our most vulnerable population, the 9th grade class. Every year 9th grade students take at least an entire semester to become assimilated to the school culture. Without teachers, this set them much further back on the learning curve. Students had many short and long-term subs over the course of the 1st semester. The class culture was poor and

This is more a symptom than an adaptive challenge. Digging deeper provides the challenge of learning how best to maintain a school culture that is congruent with its mission and vision. There is also the challenge of ensuring high quality teaching when personnel changes are overwhelming.

This is more in line with an adaptive challenge, forcing leadership to look at values, staff beliefs, and the systems in place to guide a positive school culture.

student learning was greatly comprised. Other 9th grade teachers struggled because students had become accustomed to acting and performing at a poor level.

The technical fix would have been to hire new teachers to replace the old ones; however, we had few applicants and none credentialed. We realized we had actually been dealing with this challenge for a few years: poor quality teacher candidates, late hiring policies beyond our control, and poor hiring skills by the administrative team. The adaptive challenge seemed to be to figure out how best to maintain a school culture congruent with our mission and vision while ensuring high quality teaching when personnel changes are overwhelming.

This is an ecotone they had been to before.

The identification and diagnosis phase.

This challenge directly impacted our freshman class's achievement, but it also affected our entire school culture. Other teachers felt run down because they were covering classes during their prep or helping supervise poor quality subs. After reviewing the 9th grade student data, it was clear that students were not progressing and some were actually regressing.

We made interviewing a priority and spent a lot of time completing HR tasks. We did more demo lessons and even had restorative circles with the classes. We introduced new teachers to the classes and had conversations when teachers left. We worked outside in the hallway for the classes that had subs. We began a five-week fix up when things got bad, taking specific steps to improve the supervision, discipline, and investment of the 9th grade class. I was appointed as lead of HR, a role we had never had before. Lastly, we relied on our department chairs to create lesson plans to ensure that instruction continued even with subs. For some classes, even the admin team was creating lesson plans and final assessments. We used various tools to work the challenge, for example tapping into administration time, long-term subs, brainstorming map, time during ILT and PD meetings to meet with teacher leaders, and hiring tools provided by the district.

Who Did I Bring?

The key players were the admin team, department chairs, the school operations manager, front office staff, teachers, and counselors. The administration team focused on hiring replacements. The department chairs focused on continuing instruction as they provided lessons. The school operations manager ensured that there was a sub or coverage daily for the classes. Other teachers covered classes or supported hallway supervision along with the counselors. *A core value of teaching — that teachers make the difference in the class — was greatly strengthened during this time.* We also grew in our commitment to hire candidates who shared our beliefs and had the skill set to work with our population. We challenged our eagerness to just find any replacement. We spent more time interviewing and did not just get a body into the room.

More about who to bring.

Commitment in the ecotone.

Inovation

New Thinking and Outcomes

The relationships between the admin team and our teachers were definitely challenged, as teachers often felt completely overwhelmed. Within the admin team, we grew to rely on each other more. Normally one AP handles discipline; however, we were having so many issues that one person could not handle them all. We gave up on student growth during 1st semester. We gave up on conversations about "keeping people" and instead embraced it when folks decided that our school was not a good fit and moved on.

Although student achievement did not improve immediately once all the positions were filled, the school culture shifted drastically for the better. We learned to spend time with our HR efforts, and also have candid conversations with teachers about returning for the next school year. We will hire early, spend more time vetting candidates, communicate with students and parents when we lose a teacher, and create a plan B model to use when it happens during the school year. Most of all, we learned to spend as much time with staffing as we do with instruction supervision.

Case 3.18:
Executive Director/Chief Programs Officer

The School Context

The challenge of being a founder/director/administrator/teacher of a non-traditional program with a charter school as one component of its offerings is that most people find it difficult to understand how and why we do what we do. As a non-profit affiliate of a national organization, our primary role is to be a workforce/leadership youth development program encompassing the 5 C's: community leadership/advocacy, counseling, career development, construction, and classroom. While education is important, it must go hand in hand with all of the above if our students are to succeed in "life" sustainability skills. It is not enough to have just a high school diploma; they need to develop the knowledge, skills, and abilities that society will demand of them.

Our values are love, respect, and compassion. We must and do love our young people with all the blessings (and challenges) they bring with them. We want our students to grow in their abilities to persist at whatever goal they have set for themselves. We look at this in terms of how to help our students develop resilience and "grit" so that they are able to persevere through the inevitable challenges they will face as they grow. We want them to think critically and problem solve; be advocates for themselves and their families; be leaders instead of followers; develop skills that will help them move towards a sustainable life in a job/career, the military, post-secondary education, or a trade school. We want them to think analytically about the issues of hunger, transportation, housing, counseling, access to resources, employment, and childcare as social justice issues. We want them to appreciate the concepts of restorative practices, to understand what true diversity means and how our staff and teachers support them, and to value equity over equality.

Our mission and purpose is to offer a holistic, human development approach to provide high-quality educational and occupational programs, resources, and services. This improves financial sustainability for traditionally marginalized "at-promise" youth, families, and the economically distressed communities they call home. Through the creation of an inclusive, equitable, nurturing environment, we provide culturally relevant and rigorous instruction — all within the scope of leadership development and self-sufficiency. We also promote and foster rigorous educational and occupational opportunities for at-promise people from economically distressed areas who are invested in creating a sustainable future for themselves, their families, and their communities.

The school vision is for students to successfully set and achieve their personal and professional goals, including the completion of the secondary program and post-secondary courses. Having overcome personal challenges, obstacles, and barriers, graduates of this program have developed a holistic understanding about themselves and their life goals. They have a clearer picture of what they want to learn, how to go about learning it, and how to apply this learning to their daily lives. As a result, our students are passionate about contributing to making the world a better place for their families and communities. Nothing stops them from achieving what they want to achieve.

As Co-Executive Director and Chief Programs Officer, my role is "big picture" thinking, ensuring that our programs run smoothly, and making sure that the needs of students, teachers, and staff are met. My personal vision for our work is the same as the vision for my life. *Do as much as I can, whenever I can to leave this space, this life, this world enhanced.* Other quotes that help define me are these:

> *Patience is not about waiting, but how we act when things take longer than we expect. — Paulo Coelho*

> *If at first you don't succeed, try, try again. Then quit. No use being a damn fool about it. — W.C. Fields*

> *The person who can bring the spirit of laughter into a room is indeed blessed. — Bennett Cerf*

> *Everyone has a purpose in life and a unique talent to give to others. And when we blend this unique talent with service to others, we experience the ecstasy and exultation*

of our own spirit, which is the ultimate goal of all goals.
— Kallam Anji Reddy

The Adaptive Challenge

The adaptive challenge that I hacked and worked through was the breakdown of our community culture. This manifested in the disintegration of agreed upon expectations about staff holding students accountable to high expectations of behavior, attitude, attendance, etc.

They created an ecotone based on an adaptive challenge related to school culture and how it was their own doing and responsibility.

This happened has a result of trying to meet ADA (average daily attendance) goals set by our charter school partner. At first blush, we believe it was just a technical issue, such as a new location, a radical change in demographics (e.g., younger students or an ethnicity shift), and a different open entry/exit policy. Because we were tired, stressed, and just wanting to get through the trimester, we literally dropped the ball on dealing with the cultural breakdown. We realized it as the trimester was ending, and we paused long enough to really brainstorm, think about, and analyze what the "real" issue was rather than just deciding it was the location or the students or the ethnicity shift. We looked inward and began to realize it was we who had created this adaptive challenge, not the students.

Everyone was impacted. We had poor morale, poor attendance, and lots of behavioral challenges, so we had to take action to move forward. Discussions and meetings revolved around scheduling, policy changes, group understanding, and identifying the "real" issues. All staff were involved because each of us saw the issue in similar, yet different ways. There were many critical conversations and we definitely got on the balcony to create some conflict. It would have been too easy just to fall back into the old routines. Giving the work back was difficult mostly due to different investments in wanting to solve the challenge. Those who were most vested in seeing resolution tended to really think it through — deeply. The lead teacher, transition coordinator, and directors began the dialogue before we had additional conversations with full staff participation. We reminded ourselves that an equitable shift in policy is not necessarily punitive to our students and we were okay with losing a few for the greater good of the community.

New Thinking and Outcomes

The growth in our relationships came from our weekly staff meeting/book club — we read *Wired to Care* (Patnaik, 2009) and *Leaders Eat Last* (Sinek, 2014) — which helped us bond on a deeper level. In turn, bonding helped us look at issues through different lenses (empathy, power, respect, care, compassion) and expanded our understanding of our own innate biases, giving us the ability to shift our own blind spots. We were able to look at our perceptions versus reality on any given issue. There was definitely some abdication of control and agreements not being honored, although not intentionally. More like just giving up and being too tired to fight. Some perceptions of power were challenged — but so too were perceptions of how we act and react to any given issue.

Our adaptive challenge is in the process of being changed. We will have a better idea as we move into trimester three to see if we can have true continuity around the agreed-upon expectations around what is needed to restore the community culture we have always enjoyed. We learned to stick to our collective processes and not fall victim to myopic behaviors. We did not lose anything — except maybe our minds for a hot minute. We learned how to do this work even when are we are stressed, tired, and faced with constant new challenges.

Case 3.19:
Instructional Coach

The School Context

The work at our school is to ensure that we have a culture where students see themselves as global citizens who contribute to change in their community and beyond; how they connect to the broader global issues and how they can take action. As school principal, I see my role as a facilitator and active participant in the learning in which we are all engaged. I look for opportunities for my students and staff to build on what we are doing and make it better. My personal vision for this work stems from quotes I embrace on a daily basis:

> *Be the best version of you. — Unknown*
>
> *Don't settle for being average. Soar as high as your heart will take you. — Unknown*
>
> *In a sea of troubles, focus on what's most important and value those around you. — Unknown*

The Adaptive Challenge

Our adaptive challenge was to ensure that our students are college and career ready. We wanted to be able to guarantee that students were monitored and had the support they needed in establishing their college and career goals. In the past, we did not set systemic ways to measure what students were doing regarding setting goals for themselves and being focused on them. With the implementation of Naviance,[2] we have been able to monitor and measure student goals all the way from 9th to 12th grade. This has motivated students to think about their futures and develop road maps for college. We started this process with the instructional leadership team and we pulled in student ambassadors to train them on how to navigate the program. We use our advisory students and periods to support the work. The key players for this adaptive challenge were the teachers, as they had to learn and engage students in a new process. We added the student ambassadors to support the implementation of the

> **This is a goal, assumed to be aimed at addressing some data. The deeper adaptive challenge might be that current school culture does not support a future-directed mindset and teachers are not equipped to create a learning environment that aligns with the school vision.**

---

2   Naviance is a comprehensive college and career readiness program. See https://www.naviance.com/

work. As a result, we had 100% implementation of goal setting and establishing pathways for our students.

New Thinking and Outcomes

I think to some extent we challenged our own beliefs that a system like Naviance could support student learning in a different way, which was to establish goals early on. I think it strengthened our resolve to be focused on making sure that we provide students with the best possible support for them to begin to navigate their own futures. As teachers and educators, we learned a lot from reading what goals and aspirations our students have, which also led us to begin our own conversations around developing cohesive and comprehensive tools to support them. As a result, stronger relationships were developed among the advisory teachers and the students. We became better advocates in the process. We did not give up anything in the process. I think we gained a better perspectives of our students and each other. We learned that we can make smalls shifts that have great impact.

Data collected, dialogue ensued. This is a balcony perspective to develop empathy.

We will continue to get better at this work in supporting students. We will measure the effectiveness of the results we get and have more conversations regarding the systems we have in place. I learned that there is much more learning that needs to take place. As a leader, I need to listen and focus on the work we are doing. I think it was valuable to bring others to the table to understand how to implement something new.

Case 3.20: Teacher/Leadership/Math Chair

The School Context

The mission of our school is to provide the necessary skills and support so that every student is prepared to attend college upon graduation from high school. We, the faculty, staff, and other stakeholders of our school envision a safe and nourishing learning environment where instruction is rigorous and meaningful. We are dedicated to closing the achievement gaps with our supportive, individualized attention and high expectation for academic success.

Lots of values revealed here: safe, rigor, meaningful, equity, moral imperative of eliminating the achievement gap.

My adaptive challenge focuses on how best to prepare a learning environment where student focus is on being ready to learn and improve their academic/social knowledge. From a social justice lens, our school is affiliated with the Anti-Defamation League (ADL) and practices Positive Behavior Intervention and Support (PBIS); we strongly believe in PBIS where all teachers deliver token awards to students to spread positivity. In terms of the school's diversity, all students are receiving support, such as ELL, special education, individual and group counseling, student support teams, GEAR UP, and Youth Policy Institute (YPI) after school as well as tutoring and general support during school time.

This is the solution. The challenge is…?

I teach Algebra to 9th graders, am the advisor for 10th graders, am head of the Math Department, and mentor math and other teachers. Further, I work directly with our principal as a member of our school leadership team. My personal vision for my work centers on the delivery of excellent teaching and learning instructions that benefits all my students. As a teacher, I try to support my colleagues in any way I can. I also try to support our school's extra-curricular activities. My personal and professional life are shaped by a few key quotes:

Vision.

I believe that education is the most powerful weapon which you can use to change the world for better.
— Nelson Mandela

Be the best teacher or forget this profession. Teaching is more difficult for those who don't love their job.
— Unknown

The roots of education are bitter, but the fruit is sweet.
— Aristotle.

The Adaptive Challenge

The adaptive challenge I have hacked and worked through focuses on the improvement of overall literacy among students. Last November, our school implemented 1:1 Chromebook. The school bought a Chromebook for each student and couple of supporting programs to improve overall literacy among students, which led to two major issues. First, not all students signed the contract about using Chromebook during school hours — about a 10% refusal. Second, not all teachers were willing to use the Chromebooks or support the universal programs during their classroom time or any other time. So our 1:1 Chromebook implementation was almost destroyed before it began.

The hack is literacy strategies and the implementation is in the classroom.

I chose to help our school implement the 1:1 Chromebook plan because I believed that students and teachers would benefit tremendously from having Chromebooks during school hours and more. Furthermore, I believed that I could assist teachers who needed guidance with my technological expertise. Everyone at school, including the parents, were involved. It made good sense to involve all stakeholders since the ultimate goal was to use these devices on a daily basis. Students were even allowed to take after-school assignments home under certain conditions.

Obviously, it was expensive to buy Chromebooks for all the students. The school also upgraded the Internet and bought some security and universal literacy programs. With the help of teachers, the administration carefully prepared a written contract for students and parents to sign and return. Finally, all staff voted in favor of the program. When we first assigned Chromebooks, the majority of students and teachers were satisfied, and they were using the devices properly and effectively. But those two issues — full student buy-in and full teacher buy-in — had great impact on fully implementing this idea.

Gaining full student buy-in did not require that much effort; positive talks about the benefits of having a Chromebook at school and positive peer pressure solved the problem. Those who had not signed the contract in November had done so by the end of January. Students who had not signed their agreement at first were afraid that if the Chromebook was lost, stolen, or damaged, it would be their responsibility to replace or repair it. We explained that each unit has a tracking device and only assigned students can use it. We mentioned that the school was willing to repair any reasonable damages. Another important factor that helped convince this group was witnessing how other students were benefiting from having a Chromebook handy all the time.

> **Two challenges with adaptive and technical elements: 1) a student's financial responsibility and potential impact on their family (technical); 2) creating an environment where a teacher was not "wrong" or "ignorant" in an embarrassing way (adaptive) and then finding a way to approach the teacher to support them (technical).**

The issue of teacher buy-in, however, needed a more careful approach because the main idea was to support teachers with a new tool, not to replace the teachers. Additionally, we did not want teachers to feel uncomfortable or withdrawn from implementing this program. First, we figured out who was not using it at all, then one of us in the IT group (principal, tech person, expert teacher, or I) approached the teacher carefully and taught them how to get started. The biggest issue was that teachers did not have enough knowledge and confidence

> **An adaptive challenge is emerging.**

> **Surfacing values.**

Case Narratives

about how to use computer programs in their classrooms and needed ideas, assistance, and support.

Key players were added as we moved forward with implementing 1:1 Chromebook. Teachers who were more tech savvy started to help within the department, grade level, or neighboring classes. The most important value strengthened was teamwork. We now have a dedicated group of teachers who worked hard to implement 1:1 to add another strong tool to their previous teaching tools and strategies.

New Thinking and Outcomes

We strengthened our bonds and relationships among teachers, students, parents, and administration by being able to communicate online and using technology on a daily basis. The students risked by being responsible and taking care of the assigned Chromebooks while teachers put in more time and effort to become familiar with these new programs. Our adaptive challenge has been resolved completely since all the students have now signed the contract and use the Chromebooks on a daily basis. Teachers are using universal literacy and many more programs on the Internet daily. Most importantly, we have access to mass communication with each student via school-assigned Google mail.

Practices showed how necessary and integral the Chromebook was to being successful in school.

This was a big hacking job, but it was worth getting involved to save it. Giving up and just saying no to new ideas and changes it easy; it takes sustained commitment and group effort to launch a new program and finally reap the benefits.

Case 3.21:
Principal

The School Context

Our high school is located in an urban community, population 62,000, primarily Latino, with a significant immigrant population. Only about 40% of adults have attained at least a high school education. Our program has three components: 1) school prep — focusing on high quality study habits, 2) college prep — getting them ready for college, and 3) life prep — getting them set for life after college. These components form a progression of development of the person. The Senior Work Educational Program focuses on acquiring the knowledge, skills, and experience in a career field of interest. Students begin the process in the 9th Escalera[3]; in 10th and 11th grade, they continue with Life Prep I and Life Prep II. Students explore and research their career interests and select colleges that best fit their interests. Internship mentors are identified and senior internships (Work Education) are created for their senior year. For the past three years, the school has adopted a social justice approach as we face the challenges and barriers of the current US administration. Our school has taken a lead in supporting our immigrant families and students, particularly our Dreamer and Deferred Action for Childhood Arrivals (DACA)[4] students.

Values and beliefs are being expressed through the school's actions

I have been the high school principal for the past three years. As the principal, I run a high school program with high expectations. At work, I have the opportunity to develop the school's vision and incorporate all stakeholders in its development while serving our low socioeconomic population. Using the school's data, I have been able to lead collaborative workshops to identify the strengths and needs of our organization.

Culture

---

3   Escalera is an intensive year-round college preparation program for high school students. See http://www.latnet.org/escalera-overview
4   Dreamer and Deferred Action for Childhood Arrivals (DACA) refer to US immigration status.

My vision is to empower our students, families, and communities through education. Working with students from diverse backgrounds, I have a clear understanding of the challenges they face daily in society. My leadership roles have allowed me to grow my social, community, and educational capacities. I have been able to guide students through the mental, psychological, and emotional challenges that come with transitions. Becoming a principal has really opened my eyes to the individual challenges that many of our students face and has amplified my knowledge of what students and families need educationally to succeed. As an educator, the quote that I relate to the most is this one:

> *If a child can't learn the way we teach, maybe we should teach the way they learn.* — Ignacio Estrada

As a teacher, this quote helped me to reflect continuously on my instructional practices, making me realize how "cookie cutter" instruction was not productive for our students. I had to push myself to finds ways to ensure that all my students were mastering the content. Most recently, a quote that has resonated with me is this one:

The principal is an instructional leader.

> *Education is the most powerful weapon which you can use to change the world.* —Nelson Mandela

With the current US administration, I have realized that the only way our students will have a voice in this society is by having an education beyond high school. As the school leader, my job is to ensure that our students are equipped to make changes; this can only occur through rigorous education.

The Adaptive Challenge

Our adaptive challenge was our suspension rates, which were quite high when I became principal. Administrators and teachers were always expecting students to get suspended for every reason "in the

The problem (data) is too many suspensions. The adaptive challenge will emerge later.

book." After completing the School Leadership Program, my mindset regarding suspensions shifted tremendously. As a school, we were not looking at the "whole child" and at the traumas our students were facing daily. As a leader, I began to work closely with the co-principal and our Dean of students. First, we learned about restorative circles, trauma informed practices, and teenage brain development. Second, we reviewed our discipline policy and created steps that teachers had to follow before sending students to the office. Student advisors were part of the disciplinary development process, which was an essential part of its development, and provided input on the steps. Teachers were also given professional development on restorative circles, trauma, and brain development. Third, teachers were given professional development on the disciplinary process and expected to follow each step before any further disciplinary action was taken. This new procedure saw our suspension rates decrease over three years from 45 to 25 suspensions a year.

This is the challenge — we are not equipped to meet the needs of our students so we can provide them with a positive and meaningful learning experience.

Data reveal.

The key players in this adaptive challenge were the administration, Deans, teachers, and students — essentially, the entire team. Unfortunately, this change also resulted in changes in faculty because some teachers wanted to see suspension as the only disciplinary action. Their mindsets were fixed and they refused to look at the barriers and traumas that some of our students may face. Personal values have been challenged since every stakeholder has specific beliefs regarding discipline. Some insist on immediate disciplinary action while others understand that dealing with the root causes of behavior will be of more benefit in the long run.

Who came along.

New Thinking and Outcomes

The relationships that have challenged us the most are those with parents. Surprisingly, parents also want to see students disciplined with immediate punishment. Parents have not made the connection that by taking a different approach, the school is trying to provide support systems that will eventually help students in life. On the other hand, relationships with students have strengthened because they see that we want to help and not punish. Teachers at the school have grown as they realize that building relationships with students helps avoid disciplinary problems. Some teachers have taken greater leaps into building relationships with students to support them; those who preferred to maintain a "professional distance" are no longer teaching at our school due to their values and beliefs. The culture of harsh discipline has been jettisoned, leaving some students, parents, and teachers adrift since that's what they were used to. The school has had to work on re-establishing a culture of support while still upholding specific standards and expectations.

Values challenge = parents.

Embrace the losses

I believe that the challenge will never be entirely resolved since one type of discipline does not work for all students. We are constantly reassessing our program to ensure that we support students as much as possible and equip them with the right tools. I have learned to do what is best for our students. I have learned that I cannot please every person on my team, but I can teach them that the goal is always to keep our students at the forefront. I have learned that it is okay to fail, which is important in itself, but that I still have the power to make change.

Case 3.22:
Principal

The School Context

I am the founding principal of a school within a large urban school district, located on a campus shared by three other schools. We opened our doors in the fall of 2011 and our first senior class finished in June 2013. Our school serves students from several surrounding communities, many of whom are first-generation Spanish-speaking immigrants with English as their second language. The school's demography reflects the community's ethnic background: 94% Latino, less than 1% Filipino, less than 3% Asian, and 2% other. Almost all our students (97%) live below the poverty line and 1% are in foster care. As well, our students face the following additional challenges:

- 20% are identified as special needs with an Individual Education Plan (IEP)
- 16% are English language learners (ELLs) and 45% of them have an IEP
- Over 50% are Long Term English Learners

At our school, we foster a deep understanding of the challenges facing the environment and society by actively engaging our students in rigorous academics and practical applications of knowledge. Our core values are these: *Be Water Wise, Be Recycling Savvy, Be Environmentally Engaged, Be Community Conscious, and Be College-Centered.* Family relationships and community partnerships support the growth of our students as they acquire the intellectual skills that prepare them to be environmental leaders in their communities. Our school vision is to produce generations of advocates who create healthy communities centered on environmental and social justice. Our students will be critical members of society — looked to as leaders for their fortitude, creativity, and wisdom.

My personal vision of the work is largely influenced by a philosophy I adopted through numerous quotes, including these:

Never, never, never give up. — Winston Churchill

Until we get equality in education, we won't have an equal society. — Sonia Sotomayor

The mind is everything. What you think you become. — Buddha

The Adaptive Challenge

Our adaptive challenge was to consolidate two high schools into one, specifically to bring two very different faculties together. In most ways, this challenge was chosen for me by the local superintendent of our district. I accepted it because, given the relatively small size of both of our schools, the consolidation would provide more educational opportunities for our students. I accepted this challenge because I understood that if the adults at the school — approximately 25 staff at each — were working together successfully, this would help the students also adjust. From the 2009–2010 school year to 2016–2017, the two schools operated completely autonomously and developed unique school cultures, so the challenge has been finding a way forward together.

In August 2017, we opened the school with the mandate to begin to work together. In the beginning, this was very difficult since the school we were joining with had only been informed that the consolidation was happening and that their principal was leaving three weeks beforehand. This meant beginning the year in a climate of tension and distrust. I am grateful to have a strong director who helped create the necessary level of transparency between the local district and the schools. Eight months later, we were in a much more positive place, applying to be a magnet school, holding our PDs together, and transitioning into a stronger educational institution. But the journey was anything but smooth.

Initially, some quite disruptive moves were made. All the counselors from both schools were moved into one large office space together in order to send the message that they were available for all students from both campuses. My office — office staff, assistant principal, etc. — was moved to a more central location. I had to orchestrate that conflict and think politically. I set up opportunities for people to share their concerns, but also provide solutions forward for improvement rather than just complaining. The key players were the teachers from the other school who were asked by the district to work with me, a principal they had not chosen, and a staff they did not know. These teachers were my initial concern, and where I put most of my focus. It also became clear, however, that my staff, whom I had worked with for many years, was also feeling disconnected and needed to be folded in. As the year progressed, a counselor and a coordinator left for other schools. The unifying force turned out to be the opportunity to write a magnet proposal. This created a new sense of purpose in allowing both groups of staff to envision what a true reinvention of our school could look like.

New Thinking and Outcomes
Both of the schools involved in this challenge were pilot schools with inherently strong senses of autonomy and identity. The idea of having to give up, modify, or even share this sense of autonomy was the hardest part. Both staffs have felt at different times throughout this process that this autonomy was watered down irreparably. However, as we look to the future with the idea of rebuilding our school with the best features from both schools, this challenge has shifted to a strength. Trust was initially our largest challenge; there was a sense of betrayal between the schools and the district. Choice is a very important value for our teachers so the district's unilateral decision to fold two schools into one was very problematic.

Over time, however, this relationship has shifted and grown. Our staff has had time to work together on instructional practices, draft the magnet plan, and get to know the systems in place at both schools. This process has strengthened the relationships on campus. In the absence of communication, people often assume the worse, so the most important aspect of this consolidation has been a heightened level of communication.

Since many of the teachers were founding staff, giving up the original identity of each school was a real challenge. The new challenge is to determine the second phase of this process — how do we create a new mission/vision for our newly consolidated school? Now 2018–2019 will be the planning year for the magnet school, which will open in 2019–2020. The challenge has been resolved in many ways by being the precursor to the next phase of growth.

Throughout this process, I learned that restructuring a school creates a level of pressure that can be productive but also causes casualties. Both are necessary in order to move forward. I learned that you have to provide space and time for people to grieve the loss of an identity they have held very tightly in order for them to move forward and accept the change. I learned that, as Stephen Jay Gould said, humans are "pattern-seeking animals," and that the disruption of predictability can make people feel like they have lost the ability to construct meaning in what they are doing and why they are doing it. I learned that communicating the "why" is the most important part of being a school leader.

Table 3.1

Ecotone element	From the case study	Meditations on the ecotone balcony
The initial challenge	Combine two schools into one, honoring the autonomy of each while creating a single new school	The leader had clarity of mission, recognized the points of conflict, and how values were being tested. The leader decided to seek a new identity that everyone could believe in, acknowledging the losses and embracing the gains. The leader knew that relationships would have to be created across the two school and so organized situations where the focus was on students and not on faculty identity. The faculties created a culture of collaboration that seems to have worked.
Type of Ecotone	Thrust	
What do I bring?	A vision, knowledge of how to think politically, how to strengthen relationships, how to give the work back, how to shift the focus away from what is conflicting to what is worth pursuing	
Who do I bring?	Everyone	
Values and beliefs	Autonomy, respect, dignity, student learning is first	
ID the Ecotone challenge	We were thrust into an ecotone and we shifted from looking not at how we were different, but how we could be similar in focus and mission	
The Hack: create and innovate	Created a new identity — magnet school was the hack	
Analysis — data and information		
Implementation and outcome	The magnet school was approved and now they must bring it to fruition, embracing new ways of doing things, different from how each did it before	

Case Narratives

Case 3.23:
Principal

The School Context

Ours is a small pilot school in a large urban district. Our vision is focused on creating a college- and career-going culture and developing skills around technology and communication. As principal for four years, I have been able to expand our resources, both human and financial, in collaboration with community partners. My personal work vision reflects who I am and what has shaped me as a person. Quotes that help define me are these:

> *Speak truth to power. — Unknown*

> *Supporting the strengths and passions of individuals in the team benefits the whole. — Unknown*

> *There is no room for a big ego in education. — Unknown*

> *Support those doing good work, give them credit and step back. — Unknown*

The Adaptive Challenge

Our adaptive challenge has been integrating a school-wide reading focus, specifically using a close reading strategy across all content areas. We chose this challenge because our School-Based Assessment (SBA) data and grades indicated that students were failing a content class as well as their ELA class. The change involved the leadership team, instructional coaches, and community partners who developed a plan. We presented the plan to teachers at the end of the school year in order to give them a heads-up about the changes to come. We spent three days during our summer retreat training all teachers in the protocol for close reading. We then explained how we would be integrating it into our work. The goal was to create a professional learning community (PLC) cycle around our close reading strategy. Each department would volunteer one person to go through a 4-week cycle of the following steps:

1. Have the team use rubrics to identify the level, appropriateness, and rigor of a text for close reading
2. Bring the actual lesson, including the culminating text-dependent questions
3. Bring two student responses in order to analyze student work
4. Debrief the cycle

The process unfolded in an interesting manner, starting by being uneven. Some departments did a better job of facilitating the PLC process than others. Instructional Leadership Team (ILT) leads were responsible for shepherding their department through the cycle, but many felt unprepared to lead their colleagues. The cycle was also too long as teachers did not need that much time to go through the four phases. Teachers were often unprepared, not having readings, lessons, and samples of student work. We gave up the ideas of having such a long cycle and of tracking two identified students through the entire year.

In order to remedy the situation, I met with the assistant principal and ILT to figure out what was not working and identify potential solutions. First, as a technical fix, we had support staff with leadership and facilitation experience lead each of the PLCs. We created folders for all teachers to track student work. We sent reminders to those presenting to make sure they had their materials ready to go.

New Thinking and Outcomes

The value most challenged was our overall commitment to agree upon strategies and follow through. This was especially important since we had invested in training all the staff. We needed teachers to invest in these strategies as well to really support students' ability to engage with text. I certainly felt frustrated with some members of the ILT who expressed an inability or lack of desire to facilitate and lead other colleagues. I was especially frustrated with those who had just received their administrator credentials. I also began to think about the natural leaders who emerged from this process. I think I will be replacing some leadership team members next year.

We changed the close reading PLC to only three cycles, deciding finally to make them one PD cycles. Unfortunately, due to other unforeseen challenges we now need to work on refocusing the school on some of our basic norms and agreements. We learned that you need to give things time to change, always keeping up with the other work that the school is invested in. You cannot ignore the basics as you add new things to the teacher's toolkit.

Table 3.2

Ecotone element	From the case study	Meditations on the ecotone balcony
The initial challenge	How to implement a school-wide instructional program	The leader approached the SBA data with a technical solution, close reading, assuming teachers would be on board.

Initially surfacing values and beliefs about teaching, curriculum, responsibilities of teachers, responsibilities of administration might have resulted in more effective PLCs

The adaptive challenge was never fully developed and recognized. The current systems in place were not serving the needs of students. They needed to shift their teaching, culture of collaboration, and accountability. |
Type of Ecotone	They were thrust into it by applying a technical fix without looking at how values and beliefs would be impacted	
What do I bring?	Shared a clear vision, knowledge of PLC, lots of technical knowledge. The principal brought the brain but missed the heart.	
Who do I bring?	ILT and others who could lead	
Values and beliefs	Initially not surfaced. Once the program was in place, there was a crescendo of tension as values and beliefs about autonomy, role of administration, a culture of collaboration, and effective student outcomes clashed	
ID the Ecotone challenge	Thrust into an ecotone where program was causing them to look at their values and beliefs about autonomy and the strength of a culture of collaboration	
The Hack: create and innovate	Potential leaders to lead PLC cycles	
Analysis — data and information	In progress; other foci are emerging that may get in the way	
Implementation and outcome	??	

Case 3.24:
Principal

The School Context

Here's how it all began! Our urban charter school is part of a larger group of schools that received a 5-year charter from our large school district. A co-location of this new facility was built to relieve overcrowding at neighboring high schools. We opened our doors to over 200 students in grades 9–11. In 2012, the school received a donation of over $1 million so the school now honors that donor in its permanent name.

The school campus involves six autonomous schools serving approximately 1500 students in grades 6–12 from surrounding communities. The four traditional high schools also continue to make up the local Zone of Choice (ZOC), an attendance zoning and school choice initiative that aims to provide an array of excellent, small public high school options to the local community. As such, we serve in the unique dual role of 1) a "neighborhood school" that must enroll any high school student who lives within the attendance boundary, and 2) a charter school that provides access through an annual application and enrollment lottery to students from anywhere in the state who wish to attend. In other words, students who live in the ZOC area have enrollment priority over students from other residential areas. This unique combination allows us to serve the local community while working toward building a diverse student body.

The local community has both residential and industrial areas offering mostly low-wage employment to residents. The schools sit next to a large park with soccer fields, baseball diamonds, walking trails, and playground equipment. Local small businesses, churches, and markets surround the school, offering a predominantly family-oriented, urban environment. At the same time, the area's proximity to downtown and convenient access to public transportation and several major freeways has sparked a changing demographic. In terms of the real estate market, gentrification of homes and apartments as middle- to high-income professionals with smaller households move in means that larger, low-income families of color struggle to keep the pace with the increased cost of living. Because of this, our high school has seen a drop in enrollment over the past three years due to fewer adolescents attending public schools in the area and the multitude of school options available.

We currently serve 300+ students from mostly bilingual, bicultural Latino families whose income ranges from poverty to working class. The parents' education level ranges from intermediate school to graduate degrees, with "some high school" as the average. Family composition ranges widely from nuclear, multigenerational, single-parent, or blended families to foster-care or guardianship arrangements, particularly for immigrant students.

These factors provide for a rich composition of the school community, filled with both hope and perseverance as well as overwhelming and complex challenges for students as they forge their path toward graduation and college. Without pipeline or feeder programs from high-performing charter middle schools, our scholars (we use this word intentionally in reference and reverence of all our students) often enter the 9th grade several years behind in reading and math. In addition, scholars who have transferred into the school after the 9th grade are often less proficient in academic subjects than their peers, often very credit deficient or with grades substandard for 4-year college admission. Our administration, faculty, and staff have always welcomed scholars from all ethnic, linguistic, and academic backgrounds, as well as from a range of geographic areas, to become part of our school community.

As principal, I see my role as both leader and guardian of a safe, nurturing, yet inspiring and rigorous school experience that develops leaders (adults and young people alike) and prepares all scholars for the opportunity of a 4-year college degree. We urge them to consider college just as the families of every scholar in communities of privilege would do for their own children.

A few quotes that have framed my thinking as a school leader, both of of this community and of previous inner-city communities that I have served, include the following:

On facing the harsh reality of the work in urban schools: "We can, whenever and wherever we choose, successfully teach all children whose schooling is of interest to us; we already know more than we need to do that; and whether or not we do it must finally depend on how we feel about the fact that we haven't so far." — Ron Edmonds

On my journey of learning and leadership: "We shall never cease from exploration, and at the end of all our exploring will be to arrive where we started and know the place for the first time." — T.S. Elliot

The Adaptive Challenge

Over five years, and most intensely in the last two years, with the support and guidance of our parents, our district, and others we have undertaken a total overhaul of school culture to more closely align our daily routines and practices with what we say we believe about our scholars, what they deserve, and what they can achieve. We intended to increase alignment between our mission statement, our school-wide learner outcomes, and our instructional focus. Upon further investing in the development of restorative practices at the school, we generated some new norms and values statements.

Regarding positive behavior support and discipline, our school has moved from a basic level of restorative discipline (alternatives to suspension, etc.) to a full system of positive school-culture building and incentives, alongside progressive and restorative behavior support. In addition, we've added streamlined, restorative processes for implementing and monitoring lateness, uniform violations, and cell phone violations (full school-day restrictions began last year). We utilize the Positive Behavioral Interventions and Supports (PBIS) online tool to run our incentive program as well as document behavior interventions. Last year, we also opened our weekly incentive program points store and launched several events for scholars throughout the year. Our satisfaction survey results skyrocketed to some of the highest across our district.

While we believe that restructuring the learning time over the course of the school day will lead to gains for our scholars, our newly formed instructional leadership team (ILT) is working under the guidance of the Focused Schools Development Program. About a year ago, we launched a school-wide instructional focus: "At our school, all students will be able to read and respond to complex, grade-level texts in order to achieve academically in high school and prepare for success through college." This focus emerged from a critical review of scholars' achievement data, an analysis of expected outcomes, as well as an understanding of new curricular demands for high school and college. We landed on literacy as an essential lever for driving scholars' achievement moving forward. Aligned with the instructional focus is a catchy slogan (*Read, respond, think beyond!*), school-wide culture-building routines, evidence-based teaching strategies, and annual SMART goals.

In our presentation "Three Elements of Our School's Transformation" at the International Ethics Conference last fall, our leadership team shared this work and how it has fundamentally changed our school, better positioning us to meet our ambitious aspirations for our scholars. Nonetheless, this work has not taken place without challenges. We began to tackle some very harrowing adaptive challenges about two years ago. These range from top down, bottom up, side to side, and with scholars, staff, and families. We continue to confront them on a daily basis because years of mental indoctrination are not simply undone overnight regarding the mindsets about what members of our school community can achieve. Shifting our school culture from that of a fixed mindset to a growth mindset is an ongoing challenge.

At the beginning of my leadership term, I tackled many issues using technical "fixes." Given that there were many technical problems, that approach allowed us to make substantial growth in terms of graduation rate and academic achievement very quickly. Then, we transitioned to Common Core ... new standards, new assessments, new measures, and metrics. We hit a wall in terms of academic achievement (CAASPP scores), and we have remained there for three long years. I realized, reluctantly, that what appeared to be an academic issue was really a school culture issue. We had a belief as a school community that certain students (which is how we referred to our young people at that time) were capable of achieving at high levels and would be college-bound while others were not as capable and should plan for the work force after graduation. That fixed mindset impacted our expectations of all our scholars, for better and for worse, in every facet of the school: attendance, parent participation, instruction, intervention, discipline... the list goes on. I knew in my heart — reflecting on my experience in the classroom and extrapolating to a school level — that we had no chance of moving forward as a school unless this mindset crisis was addressed.

One of the first things I did when we opened the 2016–2017 academic year is ask two questions of my entire staff at our first meeting. I started by sharing the data from the previous year, and I hinted that there were a couple of key questions we would need to consider to move the school forward. First, "Do you fundamentally believe that a 4-year college degree is both necessary and attainable for each and every one of our students?" I focused on each key word one at a time — necessary, then attainable. As expected, most responded quickly with "yes." Then I started naming some of our students, starting with our top students, and everyone agreed. When I got to some of our more challenging or underperforming students, the staff got quiet. I shared that I had responded the same way when I had asked *myself* those questions, in order to let them know that I was willing to be vulnerable and hold myself accountable as well. Then I asked, "If these students were your own children, what would your answer to that first question be? Would it be the same or would it be different? What do you think their families are hoping our answer is?" This meeting laid the foundation for us to begin a process of examining every facet of our school and asking what message it was sending, and if that message was consistent with what we agreed to be a fundamental belief for our scholars: a college education *is* necessary *and* attainable for *everyone*.

Earlier, I shared several examples of the technical work that came out of our mindset shift as a school (mission reset, cultural agreements, positive behavior support, instructional focus, etc.). Every single member of our school team is expected to play a role in the day-to-day systems, procedures, and routines that make our transformed school culture visible, audible, and palpable. It is hard work, but in the end, tremendously more rewarding. Achievement is up, behavior problems are down, and school satisfaction rates are soaring.

New Thinking and Outcomes
The most surprising, even shocking, discovery for me as a leader in this process has been uncovering the pervasiveness of fixed mindsets in our society overall and, as it turned out, on our school team. When I really began to focus on building a growth mindset, I inevitably began to see and hear fixed mindsets all around me, some that at first even came across as positive, and some clearly negative. I realized that if school team members were not willing to change their mindsets in general and about our scholars, I would need to find an exit strategy for them, and I did — about 8–10 staff members out of our staff of 35. This meant sacrificing staff who were very well liked and perceived as "highly effective" in their roles. Honestly, I have been shocked to see how quickly and profoundly the absence of specific individuals has impacted the positive growth of our school, not because they were bad people or inept employees, but rather because of their essential misalignment with what I discovered to be the driving force behind the execution of our school's vision — a growth mindset.

Connecting back to adaptive leadership techniques, I had to use all of them — get on the balcony (see the mindset issue), orchestrate conflict (ask the difficult questions), hold steady (mindset shift was the right path), give the work back (still in process), think politically (exit strategies), and holding environment (creating time and space to support the mindset shift). Mostly importantly, I had to lead by example. I had to tell my entire staff that my own mindset about our scholars was as much to blame as anyone else's, and I owned the responsibility of a "poorly steered ship" for the past few years. Finally, I had to show that it is never too late to do the right thing, to make a change, and to go for the jugular!

I learned in this process that when we are moving in that direction, no matter what the "scoreboard" says, we are always winning!

Table 3.3

Ecotone element	From the case study	Meditations on the ecotone balcony
The initial challenge	An expressed belief that all students are college bound was not congruent with the internal belief	This leader was deliberate, disciplined, and calculating in how best to lead. The leader created an ecotone of an ILT and included the school via data-driven dialogue and a willingness to hold the faculty accountable to what they said they believed in. The leader had a systems approach, knowing small technical fixes would be insufficient. Lastly, the leader modeled humility and had a revelation that training was not the answer. Rather it was about challenging the faculty mindset and engaging in dialogue to determine its impacts and how best to shift it in order to fulfill their mission.
Type of Ecotone	Created one	
What do I bring?	Clear values and a clear mission, vulnerability, willingness to ask difficult questions and orchestrate the conflicts	
Who do I bring?	Everyone; establish a new ILT	
Values and beliefs	Value relationships, embrace challenges, persist toward goals, and think globally, think beyond!	
ID the Ecotone challenge	The revelation that a fixed mindset stood in the way of creativity, innovation, and the aspiration to live up to our vision	
The Hack: create and innovate	Created an ILT and a culture where the fixed mindset could be opened up to the prospects of a growth mindset	
Analysis — data and information	CAASPP scores; the focus emerged from a critical review of scholars' achievement data, an analysis of expected outcomes, and an understanding of new curricular demands for high school and college	
Implementation and outcome	Recognition of mindset, restorative practices, new curriculum, ILT, culture shift	

Case 3.25:
Resource Teacher/Instructional Leadership Team member

The School Context

Our school started around a table in the staff lunchroom as a lofty dream to serve underprivileged students through an unapologetic focus on teaching through the arts. Seven years later, we are a nationally recognized Gold Ribbon art school. The amount of blood, sweat, and tears that have been shed on this journey is immeasurable, but I would do it all again in an instant.

My passion for a teacher-led model comes from a deeply held belief that belief itself is the only path to achieving an equitable education system that can meet the challenges of the modern world. When anyone asks me why I started our high school, my answer is simple. I built it for my kids. My daughter graduated from the school in 2016 and my sons are currently in 9th and 12th grade. The people I trust with my own kids' education are my colleagues, and I only want them to attend a school where my colleagues have the power to influence how that school educates them.

My role as a resource teacher is an extension of this philosophy. My students, students with disabilities, are among the most underserved in this country. Too often I have seen students sidelined by educators and institutional systems that do not give them the tools they need to succeed, or the opportunity to shine. As the architect of the integration program at our school, I provide an environment for students with learning differences to excel alongside their peers. As Richard Lavoie says, "Fair doesn't mean giving every child the same thing, it means giving every child what they need." Currently, it has become even more vital to speak up for the powerless and the oppressed. Among the quotes that help define me are the following:

> "Washing one's hands of the conflict between the powerful and the powerless means to side with the powerful, not to be neutral." — Paulo Freire

We must remember that the problems entrenched in our system are self-fulfilling. The outcomes are determined by the actions we have been taking. I think art is a necessary tool that gives us the freedom and courage to ask the hard questions and take bold actions. My favorite quote on this topic comes from one of my students:

> *"Art has no rules, it has no limit, it can't be tamed because it's our freedom to create."* — *Fine Arts Student*

The Adaptive Challenge

My adaptive challenge focuses on teacher performance evaluation. Since the inception of the school in 2010, it has always been a goal to implement a system of peer-to-peer classroom observations. The design team felt that it would increase interdependence, lateral accountability, and instructional transparency. This has proven to be very difficult to implement for a variety of reasons, primarily time and logistics. Much is asked of our teachers, and finding time to observe their peers on their own seemed never to happen in any meaningful way. The secondary issues were lack of training and a system. Asking teachers to observe their peers without training, or a way to frame and use the data they observed, made the process feel meaningless and a little scary. That brings us to the third issue: fear of judgment during an evaluation protocol. Being observed can be a vulnerable experience, and it often feels evaluative even if it is not meant to be. Additionally, teachers have a lot of baggage and preconceptions around observations due to past experience with performance evaluations, administrative learning walks, district rounds, etc.

In order to overcome these obstacles, we sent a team of teachers and our principal, coordinator, and instructional coach to the Instructional Rounds at Harvard. We then used our full staff winter retreat to train the faculty. I chose this challenge because it really illustrates how the whole school had to adapt and change their core relationship with observation. When in the role of the observed, we had to move from a place of "performing" for the observer to being a "provider of data." As the observer, we had to move from a place of making judgments as we observed to being an objective recorder. Since the winter retreat in

February 2017 we have done four cycles of instructional rounds and we are still refining as we go.

Table 3.4

Ecotone element	From the case study	Meditations on the ecotone balcony
The initial challenge	Implementing peer-to-peer evaluation	
Type of Ecotone	Created	
What do I bring?	Clear vision and mission, clarity of individual values, interdependence, lateral accountability, and instructional transparency	
Who do I bring?	ILT, all faculty	
Values and beliefs	Interdependence, lateral accountability, and instructional transparency; belief is the only path to achieving an equitable education system that can meet the challenges of the modern world	
ID the Ecotone challenge	Created an ecotone where a new identity was created — "provider of data" — which shifted values and beliefs about who they were and who they served	
The Hack: create and innovate	System of peer review	
Analysis — data and information	Still collecting data; attitudes have shifted	
Implementation and outcome	System is in place. We have gained a shared ownership of the school-wide problem of practice. IR forces us to look beyond our classrooms and objectively look at patterns that we find in the data. Once we identify a pattern, we take action to address the need we identified. This results in teacher-led change in the instructional program.	

New Thinking and Outcomes

As the faculty embraced the cognitive dissonance of learning and practicing instructional rounds (IR), we have gained a shared ownership of the school-wide problem of practice. IR forces us to look beyond our classrooms and objectively look at patterns that we find in the data. Once we identify a pattern, we take action to address the need we identified. This results in teacher-led change in the instructional program, which is all I've ever really wanted.

Case 3.26: Science Instructional Lead

The School Context

The mission of our school is to operate a small high-performance school that prepares all students to graduate and then enter and succeed in college. Moreover, we strive to ensure that each student will develop a resilient character and the strong critical thinking and collaborative skills necessary to become socially responsible, globally minded citizens who are an integral part of their local, national, and international communities.

I have stepped into the new role of science instructional lead (IL) this year. The concept was developed to support our small-school model as well as build up cadres of teacher leaders. In addition to functioning as a full-time chemistry and computer science teacher, the added responsibilities of the IL position include lesson plan feedback and informal observation of science, art, and physical education teachers, as well as membership in the Student Success and Progress Team (SSPT), School Coordinating Council (SCC), and Instructional Leadership Team (ILT).

Deeply ingrained in my work with teachers are facilitating and building up the Data-Drive Instruction (DDI) process, supporting the science teachers in the Next Generation Science Standards (NGSS), and providing accountability for teachers and scholars around our school-wide instructional focus. My personal vision for my work stems from a growth mindset. I tend to reflect on the importance of breaking cycles of learned helplessness. An inspirational quote that has helped define me is this one:

> *Honest discourse is the key to shifting school culture.*
> *— Unknown*

The Adaptive Challenge

My adaptive challenge focuses on ownership. In 2015, we had an instructional focus, mission, and vision that were handed down by the school's home office. Thus, the staff had little to no connection to, or ownership of the work we were doing at the school. From the department to the teacher level, each person worked in heavy isolation and independence. Opportunities to collaborate seemed like an inconvenience because collaboration, as a whole, was not prioritized and a "one team" mentality did not exist.

Deeply tied to this dysfunctional culture were low Lexile scores and failure to "move the needle" on college-going metrics. To address the low Lexile scores, we tried to implement the technical fix of having scholars read more in their English classes. Scholars needed to be exposed to more vocabulary and develop the skills demanded by the Common Core State Standards (CCSS). The English teachers were willing to dedicate 15–20 minutes of class time periodically to Sustained Silent Reading (SSR). The non-English teachers appreciated the English teachers taking on this work as there would be no impact on instruction outside of English. We even formed a literacy committee with teachers across content areas to identify high-leverage steps to improve reading and writing in all classes.

We realized a few months later that we needed to be honest about our school culture's lack of collaboration and how they tied to our instructional results (Lexile and college-readiness indicators). The literacy committee was a noble idea but there was conflict and resistance within the committee. A primary concern was that the reading and writing goals/expectations in English or history class did not align with other subjects like math or science. The department heads needed to take a step back and acknowledge that it would take "the entire village" to spark real and sustainable changes.

At this point, we formed the ILT, consisting of the English IL, the Math IL, the principal, and myself. Our purpose was to reboot: first a cultural relaunch, second a revamping of our instructional focus. A key vehicle for our work was a partnership with Focused Schools through which we built up collaboration within our own ILT, forged relationships with the ILTs of other schools, observed the work of schools who had engaged in this work before us, and studied research and data around revamping our instructional focus.

During the 2017–2018 school year, with the guidance of Focused Schools and an IL program, we launched an instructional focus all our own: *All scholars will be able to read and respond to complex, grade-level texts in order to achieve academically in high school and prepare for success through college.* With the introduction of this new focus, we also did a cultural re-launch establishing that all teachers are responsible for literacy and that we all needed to work together to prepare our scholars for success throughout high school and college.

One key shift in working through this challenge was to have transparent, direct conversations as an ILT with our principal. She fully supported and disseminated our initiatives to the rest of the school. Another key component of working through our challenge was setting regular weekly meetings. We met and continue to meet on Mondays during a common release period to check-in around our instructional focus work.

New Thinking and Outcomes
A value of mine that was challenged was to acknowledge that even though I am a teacher of science, I am also a teacher of literacy. I needed to intentionally plan for reading and writing in my class. As a science teacher, I saw myself addressing literacy by focusing on graphs and simulations. I did not really see the need to read and respond to articles or word-heavy texts such as those they might encounter in English or history class. By working through this adaptive challenge, I have come to embrace my role as a teacher of literacy. In fact, the scholars read and write as much, if not more, in my class than in their English or history classes. Relationships among our teaching staff were definitely strengthened as we established unity around a common instructional focus that we generated as a team and thus could take full ownership of.

Independence has been replaced by interdependence. Isolation and the "shame, blame, excuses" culture around data have both been lost in this process. As a school, we needed to be honest with ourselves about data for the sake of scholar progress and ensuring that they receive the best preparation for university and beyond. The challenge has been resolved but we continue to revisit our progress in our weekly Monday meetings. We continue to monitor the effectiveness of our literacy strategies in meeting our focus and aligning them to college expectations.

I am proud of the progress that my school has made. Along the way, I have learned that it is possible to implement change in a school. It does not happen overnight or without hitches or frustration but I have seen change taking root over the years. Particularly in this school year, I have noticed how the consistency in our practices across classes and our united focus contributes to scholars feeling that they can be more successful as well as actually experiencing success more frequently. I have also learned that praise, praise, and more praise is a necessary component of change. That does not mean that "the glass is always half-full" or that we are overly optimistic. Successes and progress, no matter how small, should be celebrated because these small steps over time lead to extraordinary change in the long run.

Table 3.5

Ecotone element	From the case study	Meditations on the ecotone balcony
The initial challenge	Faculty ownership of a program change	Getting faculty — who are steeped in their own academic disciplines — to see literacy as an integral component to creating citizens of a democracy is a big shift. Working with faculty to incorporate literacy strategies can cause them to think that they are "teaching content" less and will not meet the academic standards. Resolving the value conflict between academics and literacy. Shifting to accept that literacy is the highway to academic success and a path to college. There was a shift in the culture of teaching and what it means to be a faculty member at this school — it is collaborative, we all have a common responsibility (literacy)
Type of Ecotone	School — created	
	Personal — created	
What do I bring?	Instructional expertise; clarity of values, vision, and mission; collaborative culture	
Who do I bring?	ILT and all faculty	
Values and beliefs	All teachers are teachers of literacy; autonomy	
ID the Ecotone challenge	Shifting identities and how best to meet the needs of students in all disciplines	
The Hack: create and innovate	PD and meetings?	
Analysis — data and information	Scores increased	
Implementation and outcome	Relationships improved among staff	

Framework for Discussion

Case

Adaptive Challenge
1. What makes it adaptive?
2. What are some of the values that need to be let go?
3. What are some of the values that need to be brought to the forefront to ensure success?

Navigating the Ecotone
1. Identify some of the significant hurdles, then list two or three possible pathways not identified in the case and for each pathway:
    a. Identify the significant leverage points for each pathway
    b. Identify what influences each pathway may have on culture, values, and beliefs

Chapter 4

Cases for Study

In this chapter, we provide several examples for you to work through in a group to develop an understanding of how the ecotone works as a tool for change. In each of these imperfect examples, the authors are in an ecotone where they identified and diagnosed a challenge, decided on a hack, took action, and reflected. These are not exemplars or best practices. They are, however, rich examples of people earnestly working to solve challenges.

The pictorial "Summary of How to Hack" is here for your reference as you engage in the conversations.

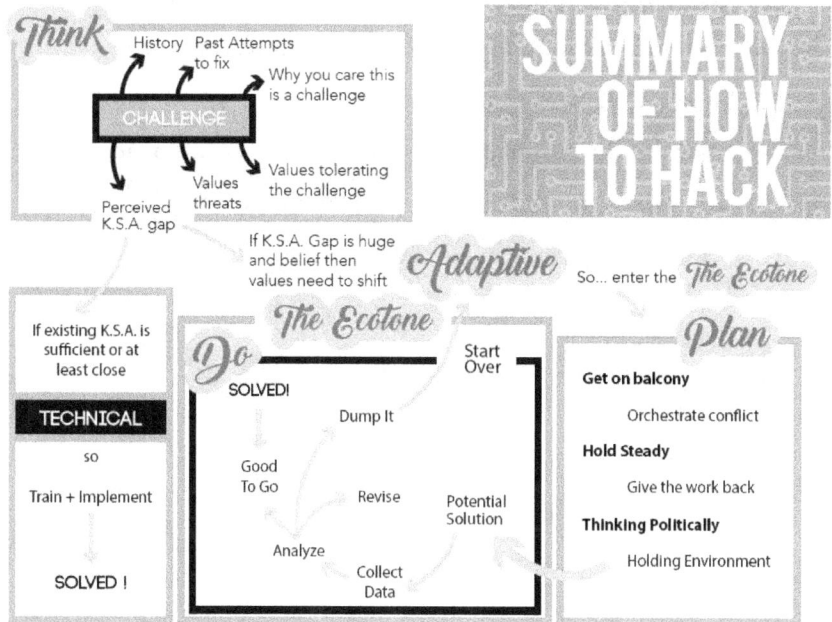

Figure 4.1. Summary of how to hack.

Figure 4.2. The ecotone process.

As you study these models, consider the following questions to guide your conversation. You may also want to make a chart, such as those included at the end of chapter three, to map out the process.

1. How did the group identify and diagnose the challenge?
2. How did they decide what kind of ecotone they were in?
3. Who did they bring and why?
4. How did the group identify common values and beliefs?
5. What strategies did they use to maintain relationships?
6. How did they brainstorm the innovation they would use as their hack?
7. What was the plan?
8. What did they discover?

Case 4.1:
Assistant Principal

The School Context
Our school is an 8th year charter school with a mission to ensure that our students are college-bound and college-ready. As the world changes, our students will be able to return to their communities and make sustainable positive change. Our students have generally been underserved in their local district elementary and middle schools and are usually 4–6 grade levels behind in reading. As a school, we are committed to increasing students' hope, pathway knowledge, and literacy levels to ensure graduation and success in college.

As the Assistant Principal in charge of Discipline and Student Supports, I am the "gatekeeper" of intervention pathways. When students struggle, I intervene and connect the student with the correct resources. When it comes to behavioral issues, students aren't suspended or expelled. Instead we pull them closer and give them more support. I believe my role is vital in bringing justice to students who have been underserved. My personal vision for the work is reflective of the following three quotes:

> *"Do you feel like you are falling behind? Perhaps, you are backing up for head start."* — Unknown

> *"Failure is the condiment that gives success its flavor."* — Truman Capote

> *"Progress is the model."* — Unknown

The Adaptive Challenge
The mental health of marginalized students is a serious challenge. Poverty often causes a lack of resources on every level — emotionally, socially, physically. Students are unable to do school work if they have emotional issues interfering. Here is a simple example. A student was referred to emotional support for concerns about depression. After a few weeks of counseling, she began to open up and was making progress. In one session, she stated that her brother sexually abused her when she was 9

years old. The counselor reported it to the Department of Children and Family Services (DCFS) who then made their own investigation by visiting the home. They concluded that since the wrongdoer no longer lived at home, the student would be able to continue living there. This led to the parent being distrustful of the school for "making things up." The mom immediately withdrew her child from counseling sessions and prohibited us from providing much-needed guidance.

The Real Challenge
At first glance it seemed that the adaptive challenge was the need for mental health services. That is already a big challenge. A secondary challenge that needs to be considered was how would parents support or deny mental health services for their children? I chose this issue because I believe that if you want to reach a student's mind, you must touch their heart. If a student struggles with mental health issues, it makes academic learning nearly impossible. The team involved the student, the mother of student, the school counselor, and DCFS. I spoke to the mom several times to get her to change her mind and let us re-enrol her daughter in emotional support services. The mother never budged, and also declined services outside the school.

The student, however, still needed help. Working with my team, we brainstormed ways to assist students without violating parental decisions. We decided to hack by creating a buddy system with students who had received help and were willing to buddy with another student. In the above case, for example, we connected the student with a successful 12th grader who had faced the same issue when she was younger and was able to speak about her past abuse in an empowering way. She took what happened to her and used it to drive her forward. The two girls have developed a mentor–mentee relationship and often speak to each other when one is feeling down. We created a whole cadre of student peer supporters. We trained these students (with parent/guardian permission) and the group has become an invaluable asset.

When mental health interventions could not be accessed, we thought outside the box and created other hacks. Now I have more interventions in my toolbox for future use. Although the mother's relationship with the school was weakened, her daughter's mental health has improved and her relationship with her mentor has grown. I had to accept the fact that the student needing professional help is going to be denied it until she is 18. She lost those professional services but gained a personal mentor instead.

The mental health challenge still exists as some parents do not want their kids talking to mental health professionals. However, I created the opportunity for students needing this service to talk to a peer who can relate and empathize. There is a hidden wealth of resources in every school right in plain sight — the students themselves!

Case 4.2: Assistant Principal

The School Context

We are a charter high school operating within a large urban city school district. The charter school is a proposition 39 school co-located on the same campus as a traditional high school. Our charter school serves a diverse base of students with a predominantly large student demographic made up of African American students. Our school vision is to ensure that each student receives a quality education that not only adequately prepares them to graduate high school but also clearly aligns them with a college attendance pathway upon graduation.

Furthermore, our school strives to help our students develop, beyond their academic grades and college readiness path, as global citizens. We do this by empowering them as active members of their school community through critical pedagogy and critical thinking skills across the curriculum. We strive to have our students graduate from our school prepared to complete the four-year college program they have chosen. As well, we train them to be active citizens within the context of their community's democracy by utilizing critical thinking praxis in their everyday lives.

I serve as the Assistant Principal of the school site. The main responsibilities of my job include pedagogy, teacher support, and discipline. First, I support and monitor instruction within every classroom. Second, I ensure that our teachers are supported in meeting the mission of college-ready rigorous instruction coupled with critical pedagogy praxis. Third, I monitor and support student discipline initiatives and school culture building. My personal vision for the work is reflected in several quotes, including these:

> *"Washing one's hands of the conflict between the powerful and powerless means to side with the powerful not to be neutral." — Paulo Freire*

> *"No one educates anyone else nor do we educate ourselves; we educate one another in communion in the context of living in this world." — Paulo Freire*

> *"If you are always trying to be normal you will never know how amazing you can be." — Maya Angelou*

The Adaptive Challenge

The adaptive challenge was to shift our school's discipline culture, which revolved around suspensions and other punishments, to a culture of care without the focus on punitive consequences. I choose this adaptive challenge because I felt it was imperative to address the discipline culture at our school in order to be able to achieve our mission of empowering students through critical pedagogy to become well-rounded, active citizens. The discipline culture at our school, I felt, not only worked against our school mission but also provided a disservice to our students. Essentially, our school's discipline culture was not aligned with our school mission, therefore it became imperative that this challenge be hacked.

Who Did I Bring?

The participants in this adaptive challenge were our school administration team, consisting of our school counselors, principal, dean of students, chief operating officer, myself, as well as our lead faculty within the instructional leadership team. It was important to incorporate not only our administration team but also our instructional leadership team in addressing this adaptive challenge, as it required an overhaul of our school's discipline culture both administratively and instructionally.

How Did We Create and Innovate?

We were able to utilize the school's central mission as a clear focus for unifying our direction in reimagining our discipline policy and practices. Allowing the school's mission to guide us and influence our discipline vision provided us with the opportunity to critically analyze practices that contradicted the mission. This critical analysis then provided us with the ability to remove certain detrimental discipline practices and replace them with practices that actually support our mission, such as discipline through restorative justice. We took this a step further and began implementing a full, wide structural change to our discipline matrix by replacing it with a Positive Behavior Intervention and Support (PBIS) matrix. PBIS training through the County Office of Education, as well as incorporating a PBIS coach on our school campus, served as critical tools in reshaping our discipline practices.

Once the administration team was able to clearly articulate and obtain the critical resources needed for this change, our lead teachers and members of our instructional leadership team were able to assist in implementing the systemic change from classroom to classroom. We utilized structured professional development time once a week to help teachers incorporate PBIS into their classrooms. We also facilitated informal faculty walk-throughs so that teachers could collaborate with one another and provide critical feedback. Coaching, critical reflection, a school-wide mission/vision, as well as continued time for professional development were all key tools utilized in addressing this adaptive challenge.

The key players were the school's administrative and instructional leadership teams. As we moved through the challenge, we brought in the entire faculty, as well as parents and students, for feedback on our process. Addressing this adaptive challenge allowed us to strengthen our mission and vision by really incorporating a crucial part of our school practice and discipline program, into our standards. This alignment allowed us to both strengthen our mission and come together as a broader team to revamp our commitment to critical pedagogy, not only within the classroom but also within the framework of school discipline and student support. Holistically, this allowed members of our school team to strengthen their commitment to critical pedagogy while distancing themselves from traditional methods of punishment in order to better support student success.

New Thinking and Outcomes

The relationship between the administrative team and the instructional leadership team was greatly strengthened through our collaborative work on this adaptive challenge. Part of working through this adaptive challenge was to shift certain individuals away from a mindset of "punishment" and towards a mindset of student support. We have successfully incorporated PBIS into our school discipline framework. This has allowed us to shape our discipline practices completely around the PBIS model, which has helped us lower our suspension rates and better support our students.

I learned that it is imperative to utilize the school mission/vision as a critical tool to bring about positive change. Furthermore, I was able to witness the benefits of a strong school mission/vision in unifying school team members in implementing that change.

Case 4.3: Assistant Principal

The School Context

Our school has about 550 students. In terms of diversity, 99% are of Latino heritage, 23 students are of African American background, 25% are English Language Learners (ELLs) ranging from levels 1–4, and 25%

are students with disabilities. The majority of our students are living in high poverty. In terms of ethnicity, our student population is not very diverse. The staff is much more diverse, consisting of individuals who identify as Latino, Caucasian, African American, and Asian.

Social justice is fundamental to our school. The entire faculty engage in restorative practices. The students participate in close reading every Tuesday, discussing articles that resonate a social justice theme. Teachers participate in ongoing training regarding trauma, culturally relevant teaching and learning, and restorative practices. Our instructional leader lives and breathes social justice and so do the other stakeholders. Our vision, mission, and goals are shared amongst all stakeholders. The vision includes a cooperative effort among all stakeholders to prepare our students for tomorrow through technology, academic achievement, and a college-going culture. Our goal for students is that they will learn life lessons and become productive citizens. Stakeholders are consistently reminded of our vision and we monitor our progress on a consistent basis.

The Assistant Principal

I began at the school in January 2018 as the assistant principal. I had big shoes to fill because of the excellent work of my predecessor. I am new to this role and responsible for a whole laundry list of a job description, other duties assigned, and volunteering for whatever gaps are left. To name a few of my major roles, I am in charge of discipline, special education, staff supervision, school safety, field trips, some budgeting, and more! My typical day includes morning supervision; daily random searches of students and lockers; meetings with parents, support staff, and other district personnel; supervision of seasonal sports; classroom observation; assisting with the development of PDs; data review; responding to emails; discipline; creating systems, policies, and procedures; threat assessments; etc. My personal vision for the work is based on key quotes upon which I reflect daily:

"God ain't going to give you nothing you can't handle."
— Unknown

"Meet people where they are." — Unknown

"All students can learn; the most influential factor on student outcomes are teachers. Building community is first." — Unknown.

The Adaptive Challenge

Our adaptive challenge was identified after a series of events. Special education is out of compliance regarding IEP deadlines; servicing and tracking time with RSP students; and EL reclassification. One of the RSP teachers was hurt in November and was still on leave in January when I started. This created a domino effect regarding compliance issues. Her IEPs became overdue because the substitute was not qualified to complete them. The students on her caseload were not being tracked. She was the lead teacher, so when she was out, everything fell apart. The former assistant principal had been a special education teacher whereas I was not. He already knew what I had to learn; I only knew laws and theory about inclusion. My beliefs were clear about our responsibility to educate all; however, the system in place was not sustainable because of the absence of the lead RSP teacher.

A New Ecotone

In a larger sense, special education is itself an adaptive challenge because we don't have the knowledge and skills to meet the needs of every student. Creating the least restrictive environment for the learning of a single student within a large classroom takes a very high level of skill. Even though the issue at hand might have been ongoing for the school, it was new to me. I would need to proactively forge a new place in order to do this work. I like to lead with an adaptive mindset, so at least I had that advantage.

Who Would I Take?

What I needed to do first was to build relationships because I was new to the school, because of my role, and because of special education (SPED). I took a hard look at myself. I did not have much out-of-classroom experience with SPED, so I had to be transparent about my lack of knowledge. I was quite vulnerable and relied a lot on the knowledge and experience of others by managing my resources — staff, local district specialists, training, and reading a lot — as I learned the ropes. I created a SPED team made up of paraprofessionals, Resource Specialist Program (RSP) teachers, the school psychologist, the English language (EL) instructional coach, the Temporary Protected Status (TSP) coordinator, the Special Day Class (SDC) teacher, and a counselor.

We committed to finding the best way forward and hashed out what we could and might do. There seemed to be a big knowledge gap about what the policies and laws around SPED and EL were. The group was also not aware of the measureable goal requirement of the district. So, knowledge was step one.

Step 2 was to make sure the right people were working on the challenge. The key players were one of the RSP teachers, a Least Restrictive Environment (LRE) specialist from the local district, and the school counselor, all of whom worked with me daily. I did not remove anyone from the group as time progressed, but I did add a TSP coordinator and an EL coordinator. Re-designating EL students was added to the IEP process by the district, which required a measurable goal within a particular timeline. This was a new expectation and my RSP teachers were neither informed about nor trained on how to reclassify EL students through the IEP process. As a team, we created a system where we could collect data on our compliance and make sure we were doing all that was required by law.

New Thinking and Outcomes

My values were strengthened by this process. My value of creating the least restrictive environment for students with disabilities was increased since I believe that an integration model is optimal for all stakeholders.

Everyone has the opportunity to learn from this environment. Teachers can learn strategies from RSP teachers, including co-teaching and co-planning. General education teachers can learn to better assist SPED students. Students can learn to be more informed about disabilities, which creates more understanding of their peers. SPED students can learn to adapt to new environments and find success in the general education classes, which will increase their self-confidence to find success in life.

I am growing as the administrator of special education because my role is forcing me to research, read, and learn about cutting-edge information and technology. Since I was the neophyte, there was only room for growth. I was able to start from scratch and build new relationships with not only the RSP teachers but the entire SPED team (aides, trainees, coaches, school psychologist, and counselors). We work well together, communicating regularly throughout the day. We also support each other, which makes our team awesome.

Before this challenge, I was used to operating from a superhero mindset. I believed I had superpowers because I never failed at anything. I acted as if I were superhuman, as if I could do it all. I had to learn to allow myself to be vulnerable by acknowledging that I did not know how to solve this challenge. Many of the policies, procedures, reports, and platforms used for the special education department I had never seen nor heard of. I had to ask specialists, aides, counselors, colleagues, and teachers for help in my new role. I am not used to asking for help. As a teacher, I was extremely confident but as a new administrator I have a lot to learn. What did I lose? I lost the cape from my Wonder Woman suit, my invisible protective shield, and I had to jettison my ego.

We are improving each day. Our relationships are strengthening because we have built a sense of trust and community. We are building a department as well as a system. We are building capacity among our team members. Each day there is a new challenge but I know that others see our hard work because they compliment us. I learned that it is okay not to know but it is NOT okay to act as if you do. I learned that when administrators show their vulnerability, others can see they are human and begin to trust, and trust builds relationships.

I learned that there is a lot to do in the world of special education. I learned it is okay to lead from behind. I learned that sometimes you must learn and grow in real time. As a teacher, I could prepare over the summer. As an administrator, I have to think on my feet. There are no prep periods. We must continually educate ourselves to create an effective, inclusive environment for all learners.

Case 4.4: Counselor

The School Context

Our school vision states that we will prepare students to be the generations of adults who actively engage in building and sustaining healthy, just, environmentally sound communities. Students will responsibly use their student voice to make articulate choices to be fully prepared to succeed in college, career, and family life while being aware of how their choices impact the environment. This vision is posted in every classroom on the Student Learning Outcomes poster, and is on the Elect-to-Work Agreement that teachers must sign each year.

This vision was written by a group of five teachers from a comprehensive high school who were part of a Small Learning Community with a social justice focus. These teachers noticed their students had a growing concern for environmental issues in their community, and that there was a lack of representation of people of color in the environmental science professions. The group came together to create the vision for a very non-traditional school. They envisioned small classes of mixed grade-levels, shifting daily schedules, a less formal relationship between student and teacher, and students frequently engaged in experiential learning within the community.

As a school counselor, I am constantly struggling with divergent demands from all stakeholders. However, one lesson I have learned is that a counselor must become a leader in their school and advocate for students and the counseling program. I also play an important role in addressing any school problems. In looking to improve the educational experience for students, I have accepted organizational roles to spearhead multicultural awareness efforts, pupil assistance committees, mentoring programs, student leadership development, and intervention programs. Because of the nature of our small pilot school, I definitely wear multiple hats other than just counselor. My personal vision for the work is based on numerous quotes that I reflect on regularly.

"Let Your Life Speak." — Quaker saying

"It's easier to act your way into a new way of thinking, than to think your way into a new way of acting."
— Richard Pascale

"Your behavior reflects your actual purposes."
— Ronald A. Heifetz

These quotes are very powerful for me because they speak of my beliefs in my work and life. I am a firm believer that my thinking should be reflected in my behavior. Having self-knowledge of my beliefs and my ways of thinking influences the pursuit of my purpose and goals. In order to be successful in life, you need to be adaptive in how you respond and thrive in different environments and situations. At the same time, you need to have systems in place to be successful.

The Adaptive Challenge
An adaptive challenge in many urban schools is that students have lost hope and do not see a way forward. While students may have a measure of resiliency, they often lack persistence. This challenge is important for student well-being because a large number of them quit the moment things start getting difficult in their academics or in other aspects of their lives. We must create students who are firm in a course of action despite difficulty or opposition. Establishing this attitude of persistence was our challenge.

Who Did I Take?

I decided that the group to create the hack needed to be students who were already persistent. Working with that group, we could decide what was needed and implement it together. The key players were the students themselves, which was important because their roles were reversed from recipient of instruction to having the power to educate their peers. In a school setting, we have a lot of technical solutions and are used to teachers teaching and students learning. However, for this particular challenge I found an adaptive solution to the problem by having students bring the change and encouraging their peers to persevere. The idea that only teachers can change the school culture had to change. By having students take ownership of teaching their peers, they were able to change their school community.

First, I surveyed those who were successful and persistent in their lives. I wanted to know what motivated them to apply more effort outside of the classroom. I invited them to make a presentation to the staff so that we might encourage the rest of the students to develop these habits. I also suggested to them that they form an enrichment club and persuade their peers to join them. A new challenge emerged.

The relationship between counselor and teachers was somewhat rough for a time. As a counselor, I had no issue with giving the work back to students and have them find a solution, but teachers were hesitant because they felt the focus would not be contextually relevant and the approach would not be rigorous. However, by having persistent students work with their peers, the relationship between teachers and students actually strengthened because students felt they were trusted with such an important task as motivating their peers. It was difficult for the adults to give up authority and control, but it had to be done.

New Thinking and Outcomes

The students were very successful in targeting and encouraging their peers to increase their persistence. Based on the results, we now have a program for incoming 9th graders to be mentored by 12th graders. What I learned is that in every community a few individuals exhibit uncommon behaviors that allow them to be successful in areas where other community members struggle — such as the students having an attitude of perseverance despite their circumstances. Despite having access to the same resources and facing the same challenges, these individuals developed strategies that overcame the barriers. By not tapping into the resources already available in the community, the opportunity to leverage them would have been missed and an inherent inequity would have emerged. Instead, using these persistent students as examples drew out their collective intelligence, applied it to a specific adaptive problem, and extended the benefits of these practices to all community members.

Case 4.5:
Teacher and Instructional Coach

The School Context

Our school serves predominately Black and Latino students. Close to 90% of our students are on free or reduced lunch. With respect to our work, we have been trying to establish systems and a school culture that is supportive to our students' academic, social, and emotional needs. We have worked to implement restorative practices and positive behavioral interventions and supports. Our vision is to work together to change the narrative of our students so they can take ownership of their futures to pursue their goals and dream careers. We want to create a community centered on coherence, equity, and shared ownership.

For the past six years, I have been working as a teacher. Two years ago, I became the math instructional coach teaching mostly 9th and 11th graders. As an instructional coach, I work with six teachers to improve their practice so that they can meet the needs of their students. I try my best to conduct observations and feedback sessions every two weeks. My personal vision for the work I do is largely influenced by three quotes:

> *"By failing to prepare, you are preparing to fail."*
> — Benjamin Franklin

> *"Educating the mind without educating the heart is no education at all."* — Aristotle

> *"We fear to know the fearsome and unsavory aspects of ourselves, but we fear even more to know the godlike in ourselves."* — Abraham Maslow

The Adaptive Challenge

The adaptive challenge is that teachers do not perceive teaching as a profession involving continuous improvement. Feedback is not the norm for teachers and most spend their careers getting little to no feedback on their practice, or on ways to improve. Coaching is not an embedded practice, nor is it part of school culture. This challenge is important to my work because I recognize that in order for me to be an effective coach, I have to be aware of my mindset towards the teachers I support. I knew that in order to take the time to listen closely to their concerns and frustrations, I would have to start becoming aware of my triggers and biases. Only when I could put these aside would I be able develop empathy and truly listen to their issues. Empathy would provide me with the opportunity to work with them based on where they were and not where I thought they should be. I would then be able to plan my conversations with them more strategically.

What We Did in the Ecotone

The people involved in this challenge were my principal, the area superintendent, the assistant principal, and the other two instructional coaches at my school. The biggest steps I have taken to work on this challenge involve my personal development of the skills of reflecting and conversing. In order to tackle an adaptive challenge, one needs to take time to reflect honestly on one's own successes and shortcomings and then create a vision for what needs to be done. Thought partners and truth tellers are incredibly impactful in this regard, especially if they understand the person's struggles and what needs to change. As the group, we first worked on our relationships, then on our mindsets, and finally on how we would make coaching a layer of practice in our school that was valued by teachers. We decided how we would coach and what the cycle would look like, then we got back together to debrief the process. We would survey teachers in order to "meet them where they were" and make coaching feel positive, generative, and completely non-evaluative.

New Thinking and Outcomes
One thing I have learned is that while school staff may change, there will always be people around who can help you overcome an adaptive challenge. Truthfully, the team that I started with for this endeavor is completely different than the one now in place, and I continue to learn a lot and continue to develop.

Overall, my values have shifted — some became more important and others less so. I am passionate about the work I do with students and teachers and value the time spent with each group. My goal to do what is right for students has helped me ensure that actions taken at my school are aligned with their needs. I don't let other values get in the way of doing what is right for students. My loyalty was challenged when it came to having courageous conversations around teacher practices; however, I now have a better understanding that such conversations are not disloyal. Instead, I am more aware that loyalty to a person is not as important as loyalty to doing what is right for students.

Some of my relationships with colleagues have been challenged because I am thinking differently. This does not mean that I care less about any teacher, but that I understand relationships cannot get in the way of helping someone recognize missed opportunities to serve students. By developing a growth mindset, I have changed; people may perceive that, which can strain relationships. Nevertheless, this could also be the chance to strengthen relationships because I can now be honest in examining our practice.

I am working hard to give up my ego. I am working not to let criticism get to my heart and praise get to my head. I understand that we are always works in progress and will always have something to learn. What I have given up does not compare to what I am gaining. Developing a growth mindset is difficult. It is much easier to criticize oneself rather than give oneself permission to make mistakes. Educators and administrators need to develop a growth mindset about the students, staff, parents, and community. I still struggle daily with developing a growth mindset as it is so easy to fall back to our comfort zones and old ways of thinking, but the struggle itself makes me better at my job.

Through this work, I have learned two main things. First, in order for a school to be successful, all stakeholders need to be supported in developing and maintaining a growth mindset. A school can have a mission and vision, but it will fail if teachers are not willing to learn and if they do not fundamentally believe in their students' capabilities as learners. Second, adaptive work is not easy for a person, so it will be even more challenging for an organization. Hiring, planning, collaborating, and communicating all help build a team that pulls in the same direction, growing all the way.

Case 4.6: Principal

The School Context

Our charter school is committed to helping disadvantaged students succeed in school. Over its 10-year history, my school created many systems to counter the disenfranchisement and academic failure that has been rampant in the local community. Our mission is to serve any student, anytime, and anywhere in a competency-based instruction and promotion structure. The mission continues by expanding our services to students with special needs to provide quality educational opportunities for ALL students with any high-needs challenge.

The staff and leadership see the school's existence as a form of social justice, although that does not always translate into activism with the students. As a staff, we need to continue our focus on our values and behaviors. The school's mission is to accept and educate all students, especially those who have not had success in other schools, and to graduate them with a diploma that prepares them for the academic rigors of a four-year university degree (or a career). We do this in order to move students out of the cycle of poverty through meeting the educational and socioemotional needs of each individual.

Over the past 10 years, we have struggled to become the school we want to be. Many programs are working well, including social emotional support, adding middle school grades, enrichment, a robust after school program, PBIS school-wide implementation, and college and career counseling. But we are still struggling in at least two areas. First, how to create academic rigor for the students in the competency-based program. Second, how to be flexible and supportive while still holding students accountable for their learning. Our Smarter Balanced Assessment Consortium (SBAC) test scores, for example, are terrible and our turn-in rate for work is only around 33%.

Being the principal of this school is incredibly challenging. While I have to deal with the normal day-to-day challenges of running a school with a high proportion of high-needs youth, I also have significant "office politics" to contend with. Because the founding administrator and counselors (now the school's directors) are still located on the campus and remain heavily involved, staff members often do not feel they are accountable to me, instead going around me to the directors. This undermines my ability to succeed as principal, making it challenging to implement my own vision and strategies for the school, as the directors keep a tight hold on what initiatives they want implemented.

These three quotes mean a lot to me, and are up in my office where I read them every day:

> *"Do what you feel in your heart to be right — for you'll be criticized anyway. You'll be damned if you do, and damned if you don't." — Eleanor Roosevelt*

> *"It is not the critic who counts; not the man who points out how the strong man stumbles, or where the doer of deeds*

*could have done them better. The credit belongs to the
man who is actually in the arena, whose face is marred
by dust and sweat and blood; who strives valiantly; who
errs, who comes short again and again, because there
is no effort without error and shortcoming; but who
does actually strive to do the deeds; who knows great
enthusiasms, the great devotions; who spends himself
in a worthy cause; who at the best knows in the end the
triumph of high achievement, and who at the worst, if he
fails, at least fails while daring greatly, so that his place
shall never be with those cold and timid souls who neither
know victory nor defeat." — Theodore Roosevelt*

*"Be kind whenever possible. It is always possible."
— The Dalai Lama*

The Adaptive Challenge

Students who come to our school have had so many years of academic failure that breaking the cycle and taking the first step just to complete work was overwhelming for some of them. All teachers report a low turn-in rate for assignments. Because of the competency-based model, the philosophy was that students should be allowed to turn in work late with no punishment or consequences. The idea behind this is that in the competency model, students need to show their mastery — and they may not have achieved their mastery the day the assignment is due. Teachers are expected to allow students to resubmit their work as many times as needed to show mastery. Unfortunately, students interpreted this as meaning that they can turn in their assignments whenever they want to. Many students do not turn in their work until the end of the semester, creating an avalanche of work for the teacher to grade. But this also ensures that the student never achieves mastery, because their do not refine their work. Year after year we have tried to address this low turn-in rate.

A Familiar Ecotone

We knew we had been in this place before; we needed to do things differently. We created an instructional leadership team for this task, hiring a coach to lead us in the brainstorming and identification of possible innovations. We surveyed teachers and students and got lots of rich data, all of which overwhelmingly revealed that simply turning assignments in later did not work.

Teachers complained that they could not tell what students had mastered because they saw no progression along the way. Students did not feel they needed to focus or study in class, thinking they would have time at the end to put it all together. Teachers were very frustrated and unsure when to move on to the next unit. Students were frustrated with teachers at the end of the semester, and had completely unrealistic expectations of how much grading a teacher can do at once. Teachers were burned out and demoralized by the lack of work being turned in. Students revealed the main reasons for not doing work fell into several categories — not understanding the work, not being interested in the work, and "being lazy" (their term).

Under the coach's guidance, the leadership team looked at the data and made decisions about next steps and actions. Our team chose a hack and took it to the whole staff. We used several PD sessions to talk about the issue and come to some collective decisions on how to approach the issue. We tried a first hack, collected data, and discarded the hack as a failure. We tried several other interventions — including a system where students who did not turn in work on time were assigned to an out-of-classroom person (counselor, coordinator, or administrator) to check in with them, create a plan, and help them get the work in. This intervention was too time consuming and became ineffective rather quickly.

We relied on collaboration, gathering and analyzing data, and support from our coach. We used our training about adaptive challenges as another tool. The key players were the leadership team (administration, coordinators, and head counselor), our coach, and the teachers and students. As we moved forward, we created a working committee, including teachers who volunteered and counselors. No one was excluded from working on this issue.

New Thinking and Outcomes

Correctly identifying the right challenge, taking the right people to the ecotone, and collaborating broadly finally moved our school forward. We had to confront the fact that our culture and ways of thinking had to evolve in order for us to grow as a learning community. We had to let go of our old narrative that our kids are just "lazy" and don't want to work. The data clearly showed two significant needs. First, teachers needed to do a better job of explaining the assessments to the students. Second, students needed a scaffold on how to organize to complete the smaller assignments while maintaining focus on the larger assessment.

Many teachers thought the kids could not do better — and many students believed it as well. Many had actually given up on improving and felt it was useless to try. Challenging them to think differently was hard. We had to give up on the idea that this was just a student issue and face the fact that the adults were part of the problem. Many teachers did not feel comfortable looking inward at their own role, which caused friction.

Our latest attempt was to create a Deadlines Committee to draft a new policy with clearer expectations about how and when to turn work in. Staff are to give clear feedback to students in a timely manner — even when the student has not turned the work in. This seems to be helping, as teachers report an increase in turned-in work. Though still in the early stages, we are struggling to get the support of the directors. The initiative is in danger of being cancelled before we can judge if things are improving. The real adaptive challenge seems to be that we do not know how to create assignments that students will value and complete.

Adaptive challenges take time, but must be addressed. It has been extremely hard to get everyone to the table and keep working on the issue. I was proud of myself for building teams and keeping the issue moving forward, even when our interventions failed. I was also pleased to see some teachers take ownership of the issue and move it forward themselves. I was surprised at the resistance we got from the directors, but we have been able to keep moving forward. On the plus side, the leadership team learned a lot and has made a point of focusing on the issue, instead of just accepting it and letting it fester. We also strengthened our connections and improved our ability to work together and problem solve. Our relationship with the coach also strengthened. We really struggled to get a handle on this issue, and are still working to improve it.

Case 4.7: Teacher Resource Support Provider

The School Context

I have been a teacher for eight years in a charter high school that is one of four schools on the campus. Over the last two years, the demographics of this campus have shifted.

Our mission says we prepare scholars for success through four-year colleges and universities and throughout their lives — as critical thinkers, skilled collaborators, and globally minded citizens. Our cultural agreements focus on valuing relationships. We support our learning community through mutual respect and being open and honest when communicating. We embrace challenges and encourage our students to be curious enough to reach their potential. We further urge students to persist toward goals and stay focused, setting checkpoints for follow through, and advocating for themselves when they face failure. We want them to think globally, think beyond, think outside the bubble, and be sensitive to individual differences and perspectives. Our instructional focus is that all scholars be able to read and respond to complex, grade-level texts in order to achieve academically in high school and prepare for success through college.

I currently work as one of two Resource Support Providers at my school. There are many elements to my job. Besides keeping our school compliant, I primarily support students with Individualized Education Programs

(IEPs) to access grade-level content using the accommodations stipulated. I also train them in life skills so that they can be successful in their post-graduate life. I reflect regularly on one key quote that has inspired me as an educator:

> *"Everybody is a genius, but if you judge a fish by its ability to climb a tree, it will live its whole life believing that it is stupid."* — *Albert Einstein*

My personal vision is for all IEP students to graduate with a plan for either college or career. All students are required to apply to a combination of private, community, and public universities. Although we currently have a 95% acceptance rate, many students have started to suffer from a "summer melt." Tuition costs and living far away from home, many for the first time, often impact whether they will go and how long they remain in college. Because some IEP students are credit-deficient, they are offered an alternative way to graduate. The CA minimum plan is based on the number of classes they pass rather than A–G requirements. Once they graduate, these students must go to community college for two years, if they want to transfer to a four-year college/university.

The Adaptive Challenge

Our adaptive challenge was that students and teachers did not see literacy as the gatekeeper for all other learning. This adaptive challenge required re-vamping our instructional focus. Many students enter our school with Lexile levels 2–4 years below grade-level proficiency. Many were indifferent towards reading — "I don't read," "I don't have time to read," or "I don't like to read" were common responses. We desperately needed a vision, along with teacher and student buy-in, to new way of embracing literacy that worked across the curriculum so that all teachers taught literacy within their content. Our adaptive challenge was for all teachers to see themselves as teachers of literacy.

A New Ecotone

Once our Instructional Leadership Team was formed, we participated monthly with the Focused Schools Network, working to create a new instructional focus. From there, our team expanded to include all teachers.

At the beginning of the 2016–2017 school year, each advisory was given a classroom library. Once or twice a week, students would have Silent Sustained Reading (SSR), where they were required to read a book of their choice for a designated time, anywhere from 10–20 minutes. Afterwards, they would fill out a Metacognitive Log, writing their predictions, reflections, and wonderings about what they just read. These metacognitive logs collectively counted towards a summative grade. Next, a Literacy Committee was put in place; they went to work to create literacy tools to be used by every teacher in every classroom. A response to a TDQ (text dependent question) was created in the form of an ACE paragraph. Students would *answer* the prompt (A), then *cite* their evidence from the text (C), then *explain* their evidence (E). This eventually became the go-to response teachers would use for TDQs and analyzing informational text. These documents became accessible on our Google Drive Literacy Folder. We also created a one-page Anticipatory Guide for teachers to introduce a new content unit.

Next, classes brainstormed possible slogans. Then, a school-wide vote was held and a pizza party awarded to the winning class that came up with the new slogan: "Read, respond, and think beyond!" Promotional material consisting of T-shirts, sweatshirts, letterhead, and email signatures all featured the new slogan, which also became part of the morning PA message. Students slowly but surely let down their resistance to silent sustained reading and somewhere along the line, we adopted a cellphone policy. With that came a Positive Behavior Intervention and Support (PBIS) plan. As students accrued points based on positive behavior, they used them to buy snacks at our Point Store. The school culture committee is planning a celebratory event where students can use their points to cash in on gift cards, art items, and movie and entertainment tickets.

All teachers and school staff were key players in addressing this adaptive challenge. Teachers were skeptical at first, unsure if students were up to the task. Some teachers did not believe that every student would graduate ready to attend college. It took some doing to get them all on board. Student mindsets too were initially challenged. They did not read routinely and couldn't get excited about boosting their Lexile levels. But reading for class was a chore and reading for content was an obstacle. Over the course of the last school year, many students developed into readers. Many found books that changed their lives. Like it or love it, students brought their books to class and read silently at the assigned times.

New Thinking and Outcomes
The teaching staff grew more committed once we presented our slogan. This, plus the formation of a "School Culture" committee and a "Best Place to Work" committee, led to a more positive school culture. Many students and teachers were able to meet the challenge and so new goals have been established. We learned that when you put a challenge in place, students will step up to meet it. Students do care about learning, graduating, getting into college, and (often) being the first in their family to attend college. They say it takes a village to raise a child. In our case, it took the leadership team plus the whole school, with some help from the community, to make this work.

Case 4.8: English Language Development Teacher

The School Context
Our school opened in 1967, shortly after the historic Watts rebellion. It opened its doors to bring hope, stability, and change to the surrounding community, and was initially a source of great pride for all of the school's stakeholders. But over time, the school became a site of ineffective teaching, low attendance characterized by violence, high teacher turnover, and a high school graduation rate below 30% in 2007. Ninety percent of students were performing below basic or far below basic on the California

Standards Test (CSTs) and only 2.5% of students were enrolled in college-prep courses. The school was put on charter management several years ago and continues to struggle in many areas.

The Adaptive Challenge

Three factors pose significant adaptive challenges for our school: inability to function in academic English, limited education in their first language, and trauma of various types. How can we meet the needs of these students, while adhering to legal requirements and the school's mission to prepare everyone for college?

English Language Learners (ELLs) and English Literacy Development (ELD) students are of great significance since the English Language Arts (ELA) status of our campus is broken down as follows: 25% are considered ELLs, 5% are Initial Fluent English Proficient (IFEP), 27% are Reclassified Fluent English Proficient (RFEP), 38% are English only (EO), and 6% are yet to be determined. Twenty percent of the population has a recognized disability with an IEP and 96% of the student body gets free or subsidized lunch. Our goal is to prepare our students to access higher education. Given that the ELD students represent such a high percentage of our school population, literacy is imperative for the overall success of our school. The enrolment of ELD students has also increased over the last seven years.

The number of English learners in our state grew by over 100% from 2012 to 2015, caused partly by a spike in border crossings in 2014. The ELD program at our school recently increased its number of teachers to address this increased enrolment. Roughly 90% of our incoming ELD students are from Central America, most from Honduras and El Salvador, two of the most violent countries in the world. In addition, children are often apprehended at the US–Mexico border and spend time in a Department of Health and Human Services shelter before being released to sponsors (usually parent, family, or family friend).

My experience as an ELD teacher working with newcomers has given me an understanding of a specific set of student needs that other teachers might not recognize, including their vast educational gaps. For example, many newcomer students arrive with little to no formal schooling; what we would call SIFE students (Students with Interrupted Formal Education). Because of our departmental collaboration, I discussed these concerns with other teachers and we were able to see that students struggling in English were also struggling in math. We then realized that this was one of the biggest groups of ELD newcomers for a couple of years. Having such a big number of students with alarming educational gaps was an eye opener, not only for the ELD department but also for administrators. We knew that something had to be done to support these students; as teachers we felt that the gaps had to be resolved before any high school standards could even be reached.

The mission of our school is to send every student to college regardless of their academic history. While the goal is noble and ambitious, it sets the stage for definite failure for SIFE students and their teachers. Let's take a look a one specific case to shed some light on the problem. A new student enrols in our school. We received the following information about him via email: *His name is Juan. He is from El Salvador. His reading and writing assessments place him at the ELD 1A level.* We welcome the student into our classes and, for one semester, we teach to the high school standards expected of us by the state and our administrators. After one semester, he fails most if not all of his classes. His teachers begin to notice and wonder about the possible reasons for what appears to be a lack of academic growth. We voice our opinion that "something might not be right" with this student. This is when the teachers begin to investigate. We speak to the student, then we make a phone call home.

We find out that Juan is from a rural area in El Salvador and his access to school was limited. He attended first grade and moved on to second. He failed second grade because he had to work with his family in the fields. He repeated second grade, and moved on to third grade. By this time, going to school and experiencing failure has caused Juan to not enjoy going to school. Consequently, he attends school sporadically and eventually stops going all together. Due to social and economic pressures, he is forced to immigrate to the United States at the age of 16.

Now Juan is expected to develop the skills outlined in the many high school level standards while simultaneously acquiring English. Juan is expected to create nothing less than a miracle, jumping from second grade to ninth grade in a foreign language. To make the challenge even more intense, he has to assimilate to a new culture, navigate his way around a tough neighborhood, deal with the lingering traumas of life in El Salvador and of emigrating, and deal with the family issues of living with a relative or a parent he has not seen since he was a baby. As for his teachers, they must prepare Juan for college in a four- to five-year period, teaching high school curriculum to high school standards while Juan's academic skills are at a first- to second-grade level at best. Juan's teachers are expected to scaffold the material and Juan is expected to graduate and go to college. Under these conditions, the high dropout rate for our SIFE students should not be surprising.

A Familiar Ecotone

My colleagues, the ELD team, and I silently dealt with this reality for many years in our own classrooms until one day change began. We had an emergency meeting to discuss the possibility of changing the student schedule because classes were becoming impossible to teach with so many students at various academic skill levels. During this meeting, we made two key discoveries. Each of us sorted the students into two groups — those having trouble with English and those having trouble with math — then cross-referenced our lists and noticed that they were identical. Students with low literacy skills were having tremendous difficulty acquiring the new language and also had little understanding of basic mathematical concepts. The second discovery was even more alarming; these particular students were about 60% of our total newcomer group for that particular year. We could not just continue teaching the way we had been doing and wait for such a large cohort to drop out, which was our school's unintended method for dealing with SIFE students.

After this awareness phase, we had to take action. This was our first hack. First, we decided to cohort the students into two groups, then create appropriate support classes to provide the basic literary and mathematical concepts needed in order for them to begin to experience success. Second, we created curriculum to match the students' literacy and math skills to their zone of proximal development. Third, we collaborated weekly with language, science, history, and math to discuss growth and potential difficulties. In order to implement our plan, we also had to reach out to the administration. The wave of changes started at that unscheduled meeting continued to grow and the results were impressive. The ELD department became the ELD team, meeting weekly to collaborate during PD time and create two new support classes, but the story does not end there.

After a semester of change, we made a third discovery. We still had a handful of students who continued to struggle because they had no previous formal schooling at all. These students could not access material meant for sixth or even fourth grade because they had not yet learned to read or write, nor had they been exposed to math in an actual academic setting. The solution was to create a third cohort and put them in a class where they would learn to read and write in Spanish. I teach this class this semester and I have students at various levels. The lessons I create depend on the student's needs. For example, I currently have two students who are learning the alphabet in Spanish. I am proud to report that they have learned about half the alphabet and are able to make simple two- or three-syllable words. I have another two students working on reading comprehension, and two more in reading fluency, one of whom speaks an indigenous language from Guatemala, learning to form grammatical sentences. In the past, these students would never have experienced success in school. It is with guilt and regret that we remember specific students in the past who would have benefited significantly from the changes that the ELD team has now made.

These changes did not come about without a great deal of effort and lobbying from us as a team. The most difficult part has been making our administration fully grasp the complexity of the problem. Initially, our work with ELD students was done mostly in isolation, within the confines of our own classrooms. Core teachers in history, math, and science struggled to identify the needs of students, mainly due to a lack of formal collaboration with ELD teachers. Through our efforts and advocacy, the

ELD team is helping to redefine what it means to be a content teacher. Our content teachers now approach their curriculum through a language lens, creating a shift in literacy.

New Thinking and Outcomes

Our results thus far have been promising. Informally, we see increased retention and more robust language development. As we continue to collaborate at this level, we hope that our changes will result in increased graduation rates, increased reclassification, and more college acceptances for our ELD cohort.

References

Adverse Childhood Experience (ACE) Questionnaire (n.d.). Retrieved from http://www.ncjfcj.org/sites/default/files/Finding%20Your%20ACE%20Score.pdf

Allen, J. G., Harper, R. E., & **Koschoreck, J. W.** (2017). Social justice and school leadership preparation: Can we shift beliefs, values, and commitments? *International Journal of Educational Leadership Preparation, 12*(1), 33–52. Retrieved from http://www.ncpeapublications.org/index.php/volume-12-number-1-spring-2017

Armstrong, S. A., MacDonald, J. H., & Stillo, S. (2010). School counselors and principals: Different perceptions of relationship, leadership and training. *Journal of School Counseling, 8*(15). Retrieved from http://www.jsc.montana.edu/articles/v8n15.pd

Bar-On, R. (2010). Emotional intelligence: An integrative part of positive psychology. *South African Journal of Psychology, 40*(1), 54–62. doi:10.1177/008124631004000106

Beyer, B. (2012). Blending constructs and concepts: Development of emerging theories of organizational leadership and their relationship to leadership practices for social justice. *International Journal of Educational Leadership Preparation, 7*(3), 1–12. Retrieved from http://cnx.org/content/m44971/1.4/

Bolman, L. G., & Deal. T. (2017). *Reframing organizations: Artistry, choice, and leadership.* Hoboken, NJ: Jossey-Bass.

Boyatzis, R. E., & Saatcioglu, A. (2008). A 20-year view of trying to develop emotional, social and cognitive intelligence competencies in graduate management education. *Journal of Management Development, 27*(1), 92–108. doi:10.1108/02621710810840785

Caruso, D. R., Fleming, K., & Spector, E. D. (2014). Emotional intelligence leadership. In G. R. Goethals, S. T. Allison, R. M. Kramer, & D. M. Messick (Eds.), *Concepts of leadership: Enduring ideas and emerging insights* (pp. 93–110). New York: Palgrave Macmillan.

DeMatthews, D. E., Mungal, A. S., & Carrola, P. A. (2015). Despite best intentions: A critical analysis of social justice leadership and decision making. *Administrative Issues Journal: Education, Practice, and Research, 5*(2), 17–37. doi:10.5929/2015.5.2.4

Forde, C., & Torrance, D. (2017). Social justice and leadership development. *Professional Development in Education, 43*(1), 106–120. do:10.1080/19415257.2015.1131733

Garmston, R. J., & Wellman, B. M. (2016). *The adaptive school: A sourcebook for developing collaborative groups*, 3rd ed. Lanham, MD: Rowman & Littlefield Publishers.

Grobler, B., Moloi, C., & Thakhordas, S. (2016). Teachers' perceptions of the utilisation of emotional intelligence by their school principals to manage mandated curriculum change processes. *Educational Management Administration and Leadership, 45*(2), 336–355. doi:10.1177/1741143215608197

Heifetz, R. A., & Linsky, M. (2017). *Leadership on the line: Staying alive through the dangers of change*. Boston, MA: Harvard Business Review Press.

Heifetz, R. A., Linsky, M., & Grashow, A. (2009). *The practice of adaptive leadership: Tools and tactics for changing your organization and the world*, 1st ed. Boston, MA: Harvard Business School Publishing.

Kang, G. Y. (2016). The value of coaching: Collaborative relationships spur professional growth. *Journal of Staff Development, 37*(5), 49–52. Retrieved from https://learningforward.org/docs/default-source/jsd-october-2016/the-value-of-coaching-october16.pdf

Kegan, R., & Lahey, L. L. (2009). *Immunity to change: How to overcome it and unlock the potential in yourself and your organization*. Boston, MA: Harvard Business Publishing.

Kemp-Graham, K. Y. (2015). Missed opportunities: Preparing aspiring school leaders for bold social justice school leadership needed for 21st century schools. *International Journal of Educational Leadership Preparation, 10*(1), 99–129. Retrieved from http://www.ncpeapublications.org/attachments/article/673/2014-3232%20Kemp-Graham.pdf

Khalil, D., & Brown, E. (2015). Enacting a social justice leadership framework: The 3 C's of urban teacher quality. *Journal of Urban Learning, Teaching, and Research, 11*, 77–90. Retrieved from https://files.eric.ed.gov/fulltext/EJ1071567.pdf

Moore, B. (2009). Emotional intelligence for school administrators: A priority for school reform? *American Secondary Education, 37*(3), 20–28. Retrieved from https://www.jstor.org/stable/i40068398

Nelis, D., Quoidbach, J., Mikolajczak, M., & Hansenne, M. (2009). Increasing emotional intelligence: (How) is it possible? *Personality and Individual Differences, 47*(1), 36–41. Retrieved from https://orbi.uliege.be/bitstream/2268/30253/1/Nelis%20PAID%202009.pdf

Patnaik, D. (2009). *Wired to care: How companies prosper when they create widespread empathy*. Upper Saddle River, NJ: Pearson Education.

Patti, J., Holzer, A. A., Brackett, M. A., & Stern, R. (2015). Twenty-first-century professional development for educators: A coaching approach grounded in emotional intelligence. *Coaching, 8*(2), 96–119. doi:10.1080/17521882.2015.1061031

Rockstuhl, T., Seiler, S., Ang, S., Van Dyne, L., & Hubert, A. (2011). Beyond general intelligence (IQ) and emotional intelligence (EQ) on cross-border leadership effectiveness in a globalized world. *Journal of Social Issues, 67*(4), 825–840. doi:10.1111/j.1540-4560.2011.01730.x

Sadri, G. (2012). Emotional intelligence and leadership development. *Public Personnel Management, 41*(3), 535–548. doi:10.1177/009102601204100308

Schutte, N. S., Malouff, J. M., Thorsteinsson, E. B., Bhullar, N., & Rooke, S. E. (2013). A meta-analytic investigation of the relationship between emotional intelligence and health. *Personality and Individual Differences, 42*(6), 921–933. doi:10.1016/j.paid.2006.09.003

Sinek, S. (2014). *Leaders eat last: Why some teams pull together while others don't*. New York: Penguin Random House.

Squires, V. L. (2015). Tackling complex educational challenges through adaptive leadership. *Antistasis, 5*(1), 15–18. Retrieved from https://journals.lib.unb.ca/index.php/antistasis/article/view/22855/26615

Zoller, K. (2015). The philosophy of communicative intelligence in cross-cultural collaboration. In N. Erbe & A. H. Normore (Eds.), *Cross cultural collaboration and leadership in modern organizations* (pp. 303–320). Hershey, PA: IGI Global Publishers.

Zoller, K., & Landry, C. (2010). *The choreography of presenting: The 7 essential abilities of effective presenters*. Thousand Oaks, CA: Corwin/Sage.

About the Editors

Anthony H. Normore, Ph.D., is a Professor of Educational Leadership and a former department chair of graduate education at California State University Dominguez Hills. Dr. Normore obtained his doctorate from the Ontario Institute for Studies in Education (OISE) at the University of Toronto. Besides his many journal publications, his most recent books include *The Handbook of Research on Strategic Communication, Leadership, and Conflict Management in Modern Organizations* (2019), *Leading Against the Grain: Lessons from Visionaries for Creating Just and Equitable Schools* (2018), and *Foundations of Educational Leadership: The Key to Developing Excellent and Equitable Schools* (2017). Dr. Normore is the recipient of the American Educational Research Association 2013 Bridge People Award for Leadership for Social Justice as well as the 2015 Willower Award of Excellence in Research from the University Council for Educational Administration Consortium for the Study of Leadership and Ethics in Education.

Antonia Issa Lahera, Ed.D., is an Associate Professor at California State University Dominguez Hills in the School Leadership Program. During her nearly 30 years in the field she has worked in urban settings as a teacher, staff developer, and site principal. She has worked in highly innovative settings as the leader of a reconstituted school and also a school that ended the social promotion of students to high school. Dr. Issa Lahera received her doctorate from the University of Southern California in 2003 in urban leadership. She has worked as a mentor for the National Urban Alliance, doing extensive work around the country and is the author of numerous book chapters, peer reviewed articles, and books. Her research is found in professional journals such as *Journal* of *Educational Administration and History* and *Journal of Authentic Leadership in Education*.

Kendall Zoller, Ed.D., is an author, educator, researcher, and international presenter with a Doctorate in Educational Leadership a Master's in Educational Management. He is co-author of Calming Chaos, Leading through the Ecotone (2018) and The Choreography of Presenting: The 7 Essential Abilities of Effective Presenters (2010). As president of Sierra Training Associates, Dr. Zoller specializes in communicative intelligence and "hacking leadership." He has authored over three dozen reviewed book chapters and journal articles spanning topics of communication, community, and leadership for educators and law enforcement. His work on leadership and presentation skills takes him to schools, districts, universities, state agencies, and corporations across the United States, Canada, Europe, China, Thailand, India, Malaysia, Indonesia and the Philippines. He has presented at the campuses of Harvard, UC Berkeley, St. Anselm College, Boston University, University of Chicago, and Loyola University Maryland.

www.ingramcontent.com/pod-product-compliance
Lightning Source LLC
Chambersburg PA
CBHW071820230426
43670CB00013B/2516